ONE THING REMAINS

Blessings as you discover the one thing that remains

Neil Call
Shannon Carroll

ADVANCED PRAISE FOR *ONE THING REMAINS*

"Midway through their book, *One Thing Remains*, David and Shannon Carroll write, 'There is such a thing as learning how to suffer well,' and after reading about their life changing, personal experiences with amnesia, I think you'll agree. *One Thing Remains* will help you be better prepared to handle adversity in your life or comfort a friend dealing with adverse circumstances. The 5 life-changing lessons they share from their experience will equip you to contend with life's challenges or assist a friend or relative in their time of need."

—**Bob Russell**, Retired Senior Pastor,
Southeast Christian Church, Louisville, KY

"*One Thing Remains* is a powerful testimony of faith. It is so much more than a gripping story; it is a testimony of the power of God's Word. You will be so blessed by their story."

—**Cathy Fyock**, Author, *The Speaker Author*

"David and Shannon's harrowing journey of faith through incredible trials is a story that will inspire you. Wherever you are in your own faith and your own marriage, this book has the potential to bring you closer to your spouse and closer to Christ."

—**Dave and Ashley Willis**, Authors of *The Naked Marriage*
and Hosts of The Naked Marriage Podcast

"Tears flooded my eyes, and my heart was moved, while reading *One Thing Remains*; and that was just during the introduction. Knowing David and Shannon throughout their journey together has been a special gift. I have observed their raw authenticity, and admire their desire to share this amazing story with all of us. *One Thing Remains* should serve as a wakeup call. It might not be amnesia, but you will face many trials throughout your life. Let their story be your story, and when you think about it, it is ultimately God's story, the story of Love."

—SIMEON AMBURGEY, President of PraiseTracks.com

"Redemptive chaos. An unexpected journey navigated beautifully by the grace of God.

David and Shannon's story proves that truly *nothing* is wasted. When our lives are surrendered to an infinitely good God, He will bring us through the most difficult, refining circumstances and use them for good. David and Shannon held onto the Word of God (or maybe it held onto them) in such a beautiful way throughout amnesia. This book is a raw glimpse of what stress can do to our bodies, and a practical tool for keeping our eyes on Jesus, whose burden is light."

—CHANCELA KEY, Educator and Friend

"What an amazing story of the power of God's Word. In the beginning was the Word, and the Carroll's remind us that's where we should return daily."

—CHRIS ROUTT, Educator and Photographer

ONE THING REMAINS

*One Couple's Traumatic Encounter with Amnesia
and Their Life-Changing Journey to Restoration*

DAVID & SHANNON CARROLL

Fresno, CA

Copyright © 2020, David and Shannon Carroll

All rights reserved. No part of this book may be used or reproduced by any means, graphic, electronic, or mechanical (including any information storage retrieval system) without the express written permission from the author, except in the case of brief quotations for use in articles and reviews wherein appropriate attribution of the source is made.

Published in the United States by Ignite Press.
IgnitePress.us

ISBN: 978-1-950710-68-3 (Amazon Print)
ISBN: 978-1-950710-69-0 (IngramSpark) PAPERBACK
ISBN: 978-1-950710-70-6 (IngramSpark) HARDCOVER
ISBN: 978-1-950710-71-3 (Smashwords)

For bulk purchase and for booking, contact:

David and Shannon Carroll
David@DavidAndShannonCarroll.com
Shannon@DavidAndShannonCarroll.com
www.DavidAndShannonCarroll.com

Because of the dynamic nature of the Internet, web addresses or links contained in this book may have been changed since publication and may no longer be valid. The content of this book and all expressed opinions are those of the author and do not reflect the publisher or the publishing team. The author is solely responsible for all content included herein.

Scripture quotations marked (ESV) are from The Holy Bible, English Standard Version®, copyright © 2001 by Crossway, a publishing ministry of Good News Publishers. Used by permission. All rights reserved.

Scripture quotations marked (MSG) are taken from The Message Version®, copyright © 1993, 2002, 2018 by Eugene H. Peterson. Used by permission of NavPress. All rights reserved. Represented by Tyndale House Publishers, a Division of Tyndale House Ministries.

Song lyrics from "Friend of a Wounded Heart" by Wayne Watson, copyright © 1987. Used by permission. All rights reserved.

Song lyrics from "Holy Spirit" by Bryan and Katie Torwalt and sung by Kari Jobe, copyright © 2011. Used by permission. All rights reserved.

Library of Congress Control Number: 2020915019

Cover design by Indurekha Ghosh

Edited by White Arrow Editorial Services LLC

We dedicate this book to our boys—Caleb, Reid, and Evan. Our constant prayer is that you will grow up to be mighty warriors for the Lord. We hope that you'll learn from our mistakes and be spared some heartache that comes from attempting to figure out life on your own. Embrace the one thing that truly remains—the Word of God—and you'll be set for life. We love you.

We also dedicate this book to our church family— you showed the world what it means to suffer and love well.

ACKNOWLEDGEMENTS

When we embarked on our virgin book journey, we had no idea what was ahead. In our naivete, we thought that we'd just write our story on paper and upload it to a book site. Super simple, right? If you've ever had the privilege of writing a book, you know how immature and wrong this assumption of ours was. This process has been a marathon that has opened our eyes and given us a deep respect for anyone who has successfully authored and published a book. Truly, no one accomplishes this task without a village of experts, cheerleaders, and coaches.

This book would look nothing like what you hold in your hand were it not for the incredible work of our editorial board:

Amy Luscher Smith – Thank you for helping us view the story through the lens of the reader.

Stephen Tweed and Elizabeth Jeffries – Thank you for your constructive feedback and assistance with fine-tuning our reader audience and ultimate vision.

Melinda Kelly – Thank you for your fresh perspective and encouragement.

Chris Routt – Thank you for helping us bring the theme of God's Word more into focus!

Chancela Key – Thank you for your excitement about this story; you lived it with us, and we are grateful for you!

Sarah Flannery – Thank you for the immense amount of time you took to go over the manuscript and suggest specific wordings and changes to make it more powerful.

Pat McKain (Shannon's mom) – Thanks for cheering us along through it all and praying with us over every step.

We owe more than we can describe to Cathy Fyock, our business book strategist and writing coach extraordinaire. Cathy, thank you for listening to God's prompting to reach out and gently push us to make this book a reality. You held our hand every step of the way, were always available, spoke truth, offered top-notch resources and coaching (your virtual retreat was a game-changer for us!), and believed in us and our story. *Thank you* just doesn't seem enough for all you gave.

Everett, you and your team at Ignite Press have been a divine appointment for us. We are thrilled to work with you and appreciate the hours that you've poured into the success of this project.

Vienna Baptist Church, thank you. We know that this wasn't the story that you had planned to be a part of either, but you learned what it means to suffer well, support your pastor, pray fervently, and be devoted to the Word and each other.

To our family and kids: We know that you sacrificed a lot for this book. Thank you for believing in the vision and calling—and understanding the time that we needed to dedicate to its reality. We love you.

To our Heavenly Father: Thank You. Thank You for waking us up, giving us the gift of amnesia, providing a miraculous healing, and changing us through it all. We owe everything to You. This is Your book, Your story, and we pray that You receive much glory through it all.

Table of Contents

Introduction 1

Chapter 1: Upside Down in a Day 7

Chapter 2: Life with Amnesia 25

Chapter 3: The Miracle 41

Chapter 4: Why Me? Why Not? 53

Chapter 5: Putting It All on the Table 65

Chapter 6: A Clean Slate 79

Chapter 7: The Need for Community 91

Chapter 8: One Thing Remains 105

Epilogue 117

About the Authors 125

Introduction

David

It's 6 a.m., the alarm is going off, and already the demands of the day are building. It's time to roll out of bed and be all things to all people—yet never be enough. It's time to figure out ways to make ends meet and somehow survive—all with a smile, of course. Can you relate to that pressure? Does reading the previous sentence cause your heart to beat faster and anxiety to build as you think about your own responsibilities and life? If so, then you are just like us. Welcome to the club!

You've probably had a conversation within yourself that sounds like, "Why am I doing this every day? What's the point? Where is all this stress even getting me? There has got to be a better way, but figuring it out takes too much time and energy." We, like most of you, made plans and adapted our lives to fit those plans. However, in an instant, life as we knew it changed, and everything came to an absolute stop.

We are your average, American, Christian family. I have a background in Information Technologies and had always been bi-vocational (ministry plus a corporate job). In 2012, God called me to full-time ministry as a pastor of our church in rural Indiana. Shannon is a registered nurse, but left the hospital in 2016 to be home full time, homeschooling our two younger boys (we also have an older teenage boy) and run her own home-based business.

We thought that we were living our dream by developing a homestead and learning to be self-sufficient. The problem is, we tried to do too much at once—and we didn't take care of ourselves in the process. Stress, long to-do lists, massive ministry demands, and few boundaries finally caught up with me. I ignored the warning signs and ended up becoming unresponsive one Sunday after church, only to "wake up" and think we were living ten-ish years in the past. Amnesia. This unexpected twenty-six-day experience with devastating amnesia turned out to be "just what the doctor ordered"—and definitely what I needed.

This book is about the journey and gift we received from a very bizarre trial. Did I just say gift and trial in the same sentence? Yes, you read it correctly.

Throughout this book, we will share examples from the Bible as it is not only a spiritual book, but also practical because it relates to every facet of life. James 1:2–4 says in The Message (MSG) paraphrase:

> Consider it a sheer gift, friends, when tests and challenges come at you from all sides. You know that under pressure, your faith-life is forced into the open and shows its true colors. So don't try to get out of anything prematurely. Let it do its work, so you become mature and well-developed, not deficient in any way.

The trial we walked through completely gripped us in a way that was unsettling, frustrating, and—oddly—freeing. At the time we had two options: become victims and sink into despair or pause and think, taking time to explore the possibility of truly remarkable lessons that could be learned and incorporated into a new way of life.

I will tell you that, in all of this, there is a point. The point is not to be perfect, but to be real and honest with yourself. If you can come to that place; a place of transparency and raw openness, where everything is prepped and ready for thorough inspection, it is there that you can discover the passion and true purpose for your life. It is in this place of exploration that you can find yourself, perhaps for the first time, and embrace what matters most.

Shannon

We know that you've been through so much too—this life is gloriously hard sometimes. We honor YOUR story and path, and we are grateful that you've taken a minute out of your busy life to decide to enter into our story.

You're going to get a sneak peek into a very raw and vulnerable time in our life. Our world was suddenly turned upside down, and we had to navigate some paths we weren't at all prepared for. What's wild is that this bizarre trial produced some of the most **life-changing lessons** for us. It's strange to say now how grateful we are for this experience. It was the wake-up call we needed, and it turned our life on a completely different course than what we had initially imagined.

There are five primary lessons we learned through amnesia that we will communicate in this book. Because these truths completely changed and gripped us, we will highlight them throughout as Life-Changing Lessons. We would love for you to consider embracing these certainties as well, and we are providing a **Reflection Prayer** at the end of each chapter to assist you in this life-changing journey.

Life-Changing Lesson 1:
Suffering is normal.

This isn't a popular message, but it's one that needs to be talked about more often so we aren't surprised when it happens to us. Suffering is an opportunity to grow, and we can all learn more about what it means to suffer well.

LIFE-CHANGING LESSON 2:
GOD DOESN'T WANT US TO LIVE A STRESS-FILLED LIFE.

You have permission to simplify your life and slow down! After reading our story, we hope that you'll pause for a second and let our experience filter into an examination of your own life, specifically how you're addressing the building stressors you experience on a daily basis. Stress is becoming such a devastating problem in our culture—PLEASE learn from our mistakes and put some boundaries and safeguards in place to avoid having an absolute breakdown like we did. Life isn't meant to be that stressful . . . it's not worth it.

LIFE-CHANGING LESSON 3:
IT IS POSSIBLE TO HAVE A RESET IN YOUR RELATIONSHIPS AND LIVE WITH A CLEAN SLATE.

As you get an insider's look at our marriage—before, during, and after amnesia—we hope that you'll see that a clean slate is possible. If you come to us after reading this book and exclaim, "I now have more hope for my relationships and am committed to offering more grace and love and forgiveness!" we will know that this book has been a success.

LIFE-CHANGING LESSON 4:
COMMUNITY IS A GIFT FROM GOD.

There are a multitude of reasons why God intended for us to live in community. Our circle of friends and family carried us during our time of suffering, and we want to celebrate the role that others play in our stories—and the role that we play in theirs.

LIFE-CHANGING LESSON 5:
GOD'S WORD PREVAILS AND REMAINS.

We want you to see how miraculous God and His Word are. We don't know where you are in your feelings and beliefs of God—and that's OK. He meets us where we are. But this story wouldn't be complete without sharing (1) how He miraculously healed my husband's brain and (2) how we saw that the Word of God transcended memory. It still gives me goosebumps to think about and ponder. We think that you'll love this part of our story!

We pray that our story brings you to that place of personal reflection and fills you with a fresh wind of excitement. Come alive, dear friend.

Please note that for the duration of the book, words set in italics will be from David, while words set in regular type will be from Shannon.

1
UPSIDE DOWN IN A DAY

Shannon

Sometimes I daydream and wonder what it would be like to have a glimpse into the future—just to see ahead to the next hour, day, or week. I think about what it'd be like if God revealed how He was going to answer my prayers, before the answer actually comes. Many of us say we'd like to know what's coming, right? I've been a part of many conversations during which we were verbalizing our longing to just know what's ahead, what the next step is, how the answer will come, or how everything will work out.

But honestly, I'm grateful that God doesn't reveal most things early. I'm not sure that I'd always want to know ahead of time what I'm going to have to walk through. We aren't given grace for future events. We're only given grace to walk through the *now*.

> We're only given grace to walk through the *now*.

And in God's master design of our universe, He planned for us to be able to fully know only the events of the past: to remember and see what happened and how He worked it all out. Sometimes He gives us clues about what's to come; though it's rarely enough pieces of the puzzle. I think that He doesn't tell us what's coming because He ultimately desires that we learn to trust.

Looking back over our experience with amnesia, I see now how God used it to answer multitudes of our prayers. However, I'm grateful I didn't know at the time that the answer to our prayers would come in the messed-up package of amnesia.

Two days before everything turned upside down in our world, I wrote the following in my journal. I was on day three of an intense Master Cleanse (ten days of a strict, liquid diet with a goal of completely giving my digestive system a break), we were in the middle of a major home remodel, and life was just plain crazy. This preemptive journal entry describes how our day-to-day world existed at the time. Maybe you can relate:

> Day #3 of the cleanse . . . It's not been terrible as far as detox symptoms so far. I was irritable with my family last night—but honestly, I think it's because my blood sugar was crashing. David has been stressed and irritable too (busy church week), so last night was another not-fun-day in the Carroll household. Grateful for a new day.
>
> We found out the drywall guys are coming on Saturday to start fixing my garage—and everything has to come out of there. UGH. It's going to be a major project today, and I have a ton of other things to get done too. Oh well.
>
> I'm reading through the Psalms while on my cleanse, trying to read and pray ten Psalms a day. As junk is cleansed out of my life, I want to fill and saturate myself with truth and let it wash over me. I have much inner cleansing that needs to

happen. Cleanse me fully, Heavenly Father. I'm grateful for Your patience with me.

Little did I know what was coming—or how God was going to answer this prayer for cleansing.

David

How did it all start? I was the pastor of a local church, and it was the week after Easter, which is one of the busiest seasons for pastors, and I had recently started a new preaching series in 1 Corinthians. Shannon and I often talk about the fact that we walk through and literally experience whatever I'm currently preaching. This week was no exception. Actually, this one takes the cake!

The week leading up to April 28 was a stressful one for me. In the middle of the week, I started having some chest pains, but I didn't give it much thought. I figured it was due to increased demands, stress, life, indigestion, and who knows what else. But I did nothing about it except try to escape and rest when I could. By Friday night, I felt truly sick and the chest pains were back. Saturday came, and I was feeling much worse: exhausted, irritable, and—I thought—just needing to get caught up on some rest, so I went to bed early. I woke up Sunday morning still feeling like a train wreck, but I decided to go ahead and lead the church service and preach. Looking back, I should have taken my wife's advice to forfeit the service and go on to the hospital.

When David says that he wasn't feeling well, he is making a vast understatement. I knew that he was not okay that morning. His breathing was heavy. He was talking about his chest hurting. Since he insisted on fulfilling his responsibilities at church, I got him some aspirin and coordinated with an EMT in our congregation in case David collapsed while preaching. Pulling on my RN background, I devised a plan for doing CPR, getting an AED, and had even instructed some friends on how to gather the congregation for prayer should he go down during the service. I honestly can't believe that I tried to coordinate and plan in case of that severe of an emergency. The fact that I was doing so should have been my sign to override his desires and take him straight to the hospital.

I remember preaching that morning on the entire chapter of 1 Corinthians 2; in verse 2 (ESV) it reads,

> *For I decided to know nothing among you*
> *except Jesus Christ and him crucified.*

Little did I know that in a few short hours my memories would be gone and I would basically "know nothing."

I remember being at the church, and I remember preaching, but it was different; it was like I was in a dream. I could almost hear myself speaking as though I was talking from outside of my body; it was bizarre. Perhaps to describe it as something near an out-of-body experience makes the most sense.

I made it through the service, but after church I was feeling even worse—my breathing was labored, I had a sense of doom, and my chest was still bothering me, so I went to sit in my office for a few minutes. Some friends asked if we would like to go to lunch, but I told Shannon that I needed to go to the ER. Since we lived just one minute from the church, we decided to run home and change our clothes first.

I changed clothes quickly and said, "Shannon, we've got to go now to the hospital!"—and I asked her to drive. She knew something was up because I never let her drive. And if you've ever ridden with her, you understand why. Let's just say that Shannon gets to places faster than I do. I remember getting in the van and pulling out of the driveway. The next thing I remember was waking up in the hospital later that night.

If David thought I drove fast before then, I basically flew on that drive! I knew it was about a thirty-five-minute trip to the hospital, but I thought we could make it. We started down the road, but he was becoming worse with every mile I passed. His breathing was labored and, about fifteen minutes into our trip, he told me that his vision was becoming blurry. I started to panic and tried to think of all my options in that moment: "Where's the closest hospital? What should I do?" I kept talking to him and praying . . . and driving even faster.

As I was still talking to him, trying to keep him engaged and with me, I realized that he wasn't responding. I looked over to him in the passenger seat of the van—and I'll never forget this moment, even though I want to—he was totally unresponsive. I yelled his name and reached over to shake him, but there was no response. I quickly pulled over on the side of the road and called 911 to send an ambulance.

I ran around to his door, pushed the seat down, and began the initial steps of CPR. I discovered that he had a pulse and was breathing, though neither were very stable at that moment. His eyes were open, but he was not home. His gaze was off to the side; nothing I did or said aroused him.

The 911 operator stayed on the phone with me as we waited for the ambulance to arrive. I kept my fingers on his pulse, ready to restart CPR if needed. I was screaming, praying, crying, begging for my husband to come back to me. At one point I remember thinking, "What if this is it? Could this be how he dies—on the side of the road like this? Surely this won't be how it all ends for us!" It was one of the scariest moments of my life.

It took about ten minutes for the ambulance to arrive. It felt like forever. They later told me that they were just a mile down the road, off the next exit. If I had gone just a little farther, they could have been with me in an instant. When I replay the whole experience in my mind, I wish I had gone to the next exit, but hindsight is twenty-twenty.

About a minute before the ambulance arrived, David started to stir. He asked where he was, and I told him that he was having a heart attack, we were on the side of the road, and the ambulance was almost there. He was extremely anxious and nervous, looking back and forth, and very disoriented.

The ambulance arrived, loaded him up, and we headed to the emergency room. I hopped back in our van and called friends and family to meet us at the hospital. Actually, I called and screamed over the phone with friends and family on the way there. I was so scared, and the emotions from standing over him on the side of the road were starting to spill out. I was panicked and still driving frantically to keep up with the ambulance. Thank God for traveling mercies that day.

I had no idea what I'd find when we arrived at the hospital; I didn't know if my husband would be alive or not, based on how unstable he appeared. God and I had some serious and intense conversations on that drive. I was living a total nightmare.

The Hospital

When I got to David in the ER, he was awake and somewhat aware of his surroundings. But he was very, very anxious. He kept holding his chest and saying that he couldn't breathe. They immediately got him in a room and started testing. Quickly, he became confused and then paranoid, saying things like, "I need to get out of here! They're going to hurt us! Don't you see they're all out to get us and they're evil?" Now it was my turn to be confused! With a background as an ER nurse, I knew this was not a normal presentation for someone having a heart attack. His initial tests were coming back normal, yet everything seemed weird and uncertain.

The next hour or two were especially bizarre. He didn't know where he was anymore, and he was convinced that everyone was out to get him. He saw his clothes on the chair and wanted me to get them, help him get dressed, and then escape "out of here." He was thirsty, but refused to drink the water they gave him because, according to him, it was probably poisoned. He was especially perplexed about the oxygen monitor on his finger, believing it was some type of conspiracy instrument being used against him. I kept trying to calm him down, but inside I was worried sick that he would make good on his threats and attempt to escape from the hospital.

A series of text messages I sent to my mom during those hours in the emergency room give some insight into what we were experiencing during those unfamiliar moments. From them, you can get a glimpse into the insane progression we lived during those strange hours in the ER:

> Getting a room. And an EKG. He's awake. Just very short of air. Had relief with nitro.
>
> In a room waiting on the Doctor. He's hooked up. Very short of air and complaining of heaviness. He's very anxious.
>
> EKG was normal.
>
> Doing blood work. He's very anxious and confused. Oxygen is normal but he says it's hard to breathe. I'm ok right now.
>
> I'm beginning to think he's had a nervous breakdown.
>
> He's talking out of his head.
>
> He's super agitated right now. I don't want anyone to come back here and see him like this.
>
> Taking him back now for CT of the head.
>
> He's calming down some. Still has no memory of the last several years. But he's not as paranoid.

> He's asleep now. Pray he wakes up with a clearer mind.
>
> Hospitalist just left. His story is so bizarre. But she said they'd worry about and check the heart first and then make sure his mind comes around before they let him go.

At one point, an X-ray technician came into the room to take a chest X-ray, and I alerted her that he was acting strangely and believed everyone was against him. He saw that she had a picture of some bones on her shirt, which triggered the intense paranoia once again. He said, "I told you they're evil around here. There are very bad people here. We've got to get out." When I came back in the room after his X-ray, he proudly confided in me and whispered, "She told me to hold my breath when she took the X-ray—but I *didn't!*"

At times, he knew we were at the same hospital where, eight years prior, he used to work as an IT server engineer. He insisted that he still worked there and was adamant about needing to get back to his department for a big project. When I saw that he was not going to be convinced otherwise, I assured him that I had talked to his boss and they had given him the day off to take care of himself. He wasn't satisfied.

This day was getting crazier and crazier! I went from thinking that my husband was having a heart attack, to almost losing him on the side of the road, to walking through his paranoia and confusion, and then finding out that his heart was checking out A-OK! Talk about a roller coaster. Due to his strong paranoia and confusing behavior, the medical professionals turned their attention to checking out his brain.

The Amnesia Reality

Within a couple of hours after our arrival at the hospital, around 4 or 5 in the afternoon, his confusion subsided and he returned to seemingly normal David. It was at that moment we discovered that he had severe memory loss from the last eight to thirteen years. I think my first clue was when, in his totally calm and lucid state, he believed that he still worked at the hospital.

> *It was at that moment we discovered that he had severe memory loss from the last eight to thirteen years.*

I tried to assure him that he didn't work there any more—and hadn't worked there for eight years, but he wouldn't believe me. I remember him saying, "I just *know* I still work here! *This* is my place of employment!" He would shake his head when I told him that it wasn't. When I told him that he was a pastor, he thought *I* was out of *my* mind! "You can't be for real!" was a common response in this conversation.

When I realized that he was living in the past, I started updating him very quickly on our life to see if anything triggered his memories:

"How old do you think our boys are?" I asked.

"I don't know, but the little ones are in car seats, right?" he replied.

"No, they're nine and ten now, and Caleb is sixteen. Do you know where we live?"

"We still live in Henryville; in the house we built right after we got married."

"No, we moved from there six years ago and now live in Scottsburg, just one minute from our church, where you're the pastor," I corrected.

He was blown away by it all and couldn't grasp any of it. The picture was becoming clearer—we were dealing with a significant and sudden amnesia.

At that moment, I didn't know what to think about all of this. I was in a total fog, trying to grasp if this was even real life. As Shannon was trying to orient me to our life, I couldn't wrap my mind around any of it. I was experiencing anxiety, fear, doubt, bewilderment, and complete confusion—all at the same time. I felt trapped.

> I was in a total fog, trying to grasp if this was even real life.

We determined the memory loss to be eight years since our youngest son, Evan, was nine at the time and David remembered him as a baby. However, he had zero recollection of the church where he had pastored for the last thirteen years, and details in between those eight to thirteen years were fuzzy. He remembered all of life before the thirteen years, but none of it past the eight years. No one could figure out what happened to this healthy guy on the side of the road that Sunday and how he ended up with such a strange, severe amnesia.

Now here's the interesting thing. First Corinthians 2:5 (ESV), which I preached about earlier that Sunday morning, says:

So that your faith might not rest in the wisdom of men, but in the power of God.

Think about this for a minute: How would this whole story have turned out differently if any of the medical professionals had said, "Oh! We know exactly what this is!"? But one by one, each professional came in—the psychiatrist, the cardiologist, the neurologist, the primary care physician—and they all scratched their heads and said that they didn't have a clue what was happening. If they had known the specific medical cause, people would have reacted differently. But when none of the so-called educated professionals knew, who else was there to turn to but God?

> But when none of the so-called educated professionals knew, who else was there to turn to but God?

When he got settled in his hospital room that first night and I finally left to go sleep at my parent's house (after training him how to use his iPhone to call me if he needed anything), I remember being completely dumbfounded by and drained from the events of that day. My brain didn't know how to process it all, and I was totally overwhelmed. I had no explanations for any of it; I wasn't even sure what happened. I had the thought, "I'm going to eventually need counseling from all of today's trauma."

The two-day hospital stay was a continuation of the roller coaster. We were searching for answers, hoping that his brain would pop back into gear at any moment. We were grasping for common ground while orienting David to present day life. It was a twilight-zone experience for all of us, trying to wrap our brains around whatever was happening.

In the midst of all the chaos, some beautiful interactions took place and we started to get a glimpse of God's hand.

The tech in the MRI department commented to David, "Well, the bright side is God has given you a clean, fresh slate in life. That's a gift a lot of people would like." Her words of encouragement and life have stayed with us to this day! Isn't it just like God to plant messengers of hope in the most unexpected places?

Even though I tried to remain strong on the outside, my insides were a mess. This disturbing experience was taking its toll, and I didn't know which way was up anymore. While sitting in the hospital room, I "randomly" received a text from a dear friend. She had no idea that we were in the hospital or what was going on (we hadn't actually talked in several months) but she said that she had this strong impression to reach out to me.

As it turns out, she was working at the hospital at that moment and was able to come down and visit with me at the exact time David was out of the room for multiple tests. God sent her to me as an angel that day! I was able to share the story with her and express my whirlwind of emotions and fears. She gave me a safe place to cry and she offered hope and such sweet encouragement. It was a gift straight from Heaven in the middle of a terrible and scary hospital stay. God was with us and already providing for our every need.

You may have heard the phrase, "You don't know what you don't know." I needed to find answers, I was desperate to find answers. How is it possible to have so many thoughts in your brain and, at the same time, know that there was an inaccessible vault storing years of memories?

My mind was working overtime to resolve whatever had caused this amnesia.

One night in the hospital, while trying to sleep, I had the first of three vivid dreams. In it, I was walking down a dimly lit hallway of what looked like an office building. All of the doors on each side of the hallway were locked, and the lights in each room were off. At the end of the hallway was another door, which was facing me. Behind this door was a brilliant light, and I knew that, even in my dream, behind this door were the answers my brain needed.

I approached the door and reached for the handle, anticipating with excitement the revelation—and maybe even healing—that awaited on the other side of the door. In that moment, the lights to my hospital room came on and a voice called out, awakening me from my slumber, "Phlebotomy!"

NO! NO! NO! I was so close to finding answers and now so frustrated that I had been prematurely awakened. Not only did I not open the door in my dream, not only did I not get any answers, but I also got stuck with yet another needle.

The next morning, a well-meaning psychiatrist came into my room and asked several questions. She offered to prescribe a medication for depression. I immediately responded, "I'm not depressed. Frustrated, yes. Depressed, no."

Later the same day, a neurologist came to my room and asked Shannon to leave for a bit. He then proceeded to ask about the state of my marriage. I guess he was trying to find the root of my stress or a possible cause for my amnesia. He began by asking:

"What's really going on here? How's everything between you and your wife?"

"I guess it's good. That might be a good question to ask her since I don't really know!"

"How are your finances?" he asked.

"That's another great question I don't have the answer to."

He then asked if anything was bothering me. I broke down in tears.

"What is it?" he asked.

"My kids!"

"What about them?"

"I remember them as babies, and they just came to visit me a little bit ago. I'm just having such a hard time with it all."

The younger boys visiting David in the hospital was a pivotal event for all of us. In that moment, David's amnesia was definite, clear, and blaring at us like a neon road sign. We couldn't deny this reality any more. After we got home, I asked the boys about their thoughts from when they first saw their dad in the hospital. Apparently, Grandma had told them that their dad's memories were gone and he had amnesia. Reid (ten at the time) knew about the word *amnesia* from a *Legends of Zelda* video game. Evan (nine at the time) had never heard of it. They quickly understood its full meaning.

Reid recounts, "It all felt so weird because I expected him to remember pretty much everything. I only expected him to forget one or two little things, and he forgot like eight years! I tried to show him a ton of pictures and videos to help him remember, but that didn't help. There was just this feeling in the air like something was wrong—this sense that something isn't OK right now."

Evan also thought David had just forgotten a couple of things, but left that hospital visit in tears. "It was really weird, I guess because I had never seen Dad in the hospital. He just looked so stressed."

Our oldest, Caleb (sixteen at the time), finally saw his dad once David arrived home. His first impression was mixed, "I was glad he was alive, but I was also scared."

After all the poking and prodding and all of the tests were completed, everything came back clean. The general consensus was that years of cumulative stress contributed to this episode. The neurologist said that my memories could come back in a day, a week, a year, or never. He instructed us to go home, live our life, and, if we needed to, give him a call. With that, they discharged me from the hospital.

> "I was glad he was alive, but I was also scared."

Daily Life with Amnesia

The ride home from the hospital was strange. I recognized several buildings and roads from life "before," but many things were new. I remembered the house that we had previously lived in, but our current house was completely foreign to me. When Shannon took me inside, it was like walking into it for the first time. It didn't feel like home. I didn't know where my toothbrush was. I didn't know where my clothes were. And I kept referring to it as if it was Shannon's house.

Early on, I noticed that the hot water heater had a leak, so I informed Shannon, "YOUR hot water heater is leaking. YOU might want to call YOUR plumber."

She retorted, "Well, OUR plumber's contact information is in YOUR phone." Situations like that one occurred every day and it was hard when they did. Another time, Shannon asked, "Can you help me put some dishes away?"

I replied, "Sure! Where do they all go?" It was frustrating.

Trying to get used to "normal" was difficult. Every task was a reminder of what I did not know. I looked in the mirror and wondered, "When did I get gray hair?" I looked at Shannon's iPhone and said, "What in the world is that? It doesn't look like a Blackberry!" (For those of you who don't know, a Blackberry was a popular phone and multitasking device from the early 2000s.)

Daily life with amnesia was at times comical, but other times it was frustrating, overwhelming, and even irritating. It's pretty hard to wrap your brain around the millions of layers affected by amnesia. Maybe some of these conversations will give you a glimpse into what we were experiencing multiple times a day:

Me: Hey, do you remember the businessman Donald Trump?

David: Yes, I remember him.

Me: Well he's now our president of the United States!

David: NO WAY! You're kidding me, right?!

Me: So I don't work at the hospital anymore. I'm home full time and work with Young Living Essential Oils.

David: What's that?

Me: A network marketing company that sells essential oils and natural products.

David: Are you kidding me again?! You didn't like network marketing! And what in the world are essential oils?!

Me: Well, we love it now! It's changed our life, and it's allowing me to work from home and help others be more well.

David: Interesting. (His new favorite word!)

Side note: Our family had changed a ton over ten-plus years! It was a lot to take in at once—our gluten free diet, using all the essential oils for ALL things, having "all-natural" toothpaste and shampoo, and me being on a cleanse. David tells me now that seeing our massive lifestyle changes was one of the hardest things to grasp; he felt like he was suddenly inserted into a completely different family than the one he remembered.

David: Why do we have twenty chickens?! I don't even like chickens and I can't eat them?! (He is allergic to poultry!)

Me: The chickens were your idea . . .

Within a day or so of being home, I sent this message to some friends:

> We desperately need God's help. We are home, which is wonderful. But everything here is "new," so life is extremely overwhelming. We are figuring it out and adjusting, being honest, crying, laughing, resting, trusting...but it's hard, friends. He wanted to go look around the church. He found his Bible and sermon notes, which he doesn't remember at all. Praying God restores him to preaching when it's time!

As I watched him exploring the pulpit and rediscovering his Bible, I prayed this verse (John 14:26 ESV) as a promise:

> But the Helper, the Holy Spirit, whom the Father will send in my name, he will teach you all things and bring to your remembrance all that I have said to you.

As we attempted to integrate back into life, I saw how tired David was. His brain would get "full" easily, and he would have to step away. Imagine that every single second you're absorbing brand-new information and you have a limited context to know what to do with it all. His attitude was amazing and, even though he was scared out of his mind (pun intended!), he demonstrated peace and a quiet spirit. He spent a lot of time reading in the Word, learning about life and our boys, jumping in to do what he could, resting, and researching brain health.

Homelife was a reminder of everything I had missed. My boys were older—much older—than I remembered. My oldest son was sixteen and had a full beard. When did that happen? Everything was a mental overload and wore me out easily. My boys were asking question after question, and I tried to describe amnesia to them using the analogy that it was like someone took an ice cream scoop and scooped out years of my memories, that they were just gone. I prayed to God, "Please help me!"

I know this change was difficult for my family. They were all loving, but I could see their stress. Shannon was doing her best to handle everything when, normally, we would have shared responsibilities. This period was an emotional roller coaster for everyone. I felt helpless; I couldn't do anything. Yet we were blessed and together.

It was also overwhelming to take in our homestead. Everywhere I looked, there was something that needed to be done: fields needed to be mowed, our garden needed attention, our henhouse needed repairs. On and on it went. I thought to myself, "Why are we doing all of this?" I wanted to get away from it all.

Nighttime did not always bring relief. My mind was racing and processing all through the night. One evening, shortly after coming home from the hospital, I had a second vivid dream. In the dream, I was standing in an IT server room, similar to where I used to work. There was row after row of server racks, all filled with servers that had errors. I was walking down each row, cataloging all of the errors in order to prioritize which ones needed to be addressed first. Somehow, I knew it was a dream and that all of it was related to my mind trying to sort everything out. It didn't bring me any answers, and I woke up exhausted. This pattern of exhaustion from trying to sort it all out in my mind was becoming a new daily reality.

Shannon thought it would be good to get me out of the house, so she took me on a grocery trip. On the way to the store, we had a conversation about what to do if we encountered someone from our life and I didn't recognize them. I laughed and thought, "This is really not a big deal. I'm not going to know anybody even if they know me!" What a strange conversation to be having . . . While at the store, a friend from church approached us. I had no idea who he was, but I shook his hand and tried to wear a smile. Shannon introduced me, and we quickly moved on. As I processed that awkward encounter, I thought, "I can do this." On one hand, it should have been no big deal. On the other hand, it was totally freaking me out.

It was all such a radical, bizarre experience—like living in a movie. I knew that God was going to use it big-time; it was obvious that He was doing a new thing in us, even when we didn't understand any of it.

Reflection Prayer

Heavenly Father, sometimes life can throw unexpected curve balls that attempt to shake me. Thank You for carrying me when I am confused and burdened and uncertain. Help me to stay anchored in You, no matter what I'm going through in my life, knowing that You are with me.

2
LIFE WITH AMNESIA

Daily life with amnesia was a peculiar thing. We had both hilarious moments and overwhelming moments—times of sweet peace and times of deep anxiety. We recognize that our journey is not something most people will ever experience in their own lifetime (praise God!), so we want to give you a glimpse into what dissociative retrograde amnesia looked like and how each of us in the family reacted to its effects.

Here's a text I sent to some friends during our first week at home. It captures the roller coaster of our new life:

> Morning, friends! Every day we adjust a little bit more to life with amnesia. David spent more time at the church last night - I was able to remember his computer password (from something he told me years ago!) and he enjoyed putzing around on it. He spent a few minutes looking through our church directory until he got overwhelmed with all

> the people he doesn't know anymore. Today he's reading a book about brain health. He just now remembered something about our dishwasher!! (We have a repair guy here, and David recalled something from when it was installed!) That made his day. The memories are in there. I am starting to sense that God needs to get our attention for a significant change in how we had previously done life. I think God will give us a season of rest and renewal first – before or as part of the healing. We are being very still and trusting God. I know David is struggling big time - but God's grace is sufficient. So grateful for your prayers.

I had a hard time figuring out why we had to walk through such a radical and bizarre trial. I had to remind myself that there's no condemnation with the Lord (see Rom. 8:1), but I struggled with a lot of guilt over how we had previously been so stubborn and stuck that we couldn't hear or obey God's voice. I wanted to make sure that we didn't waste these lessons or this experience; it had to count for something.

With David's fresh perspective on our life, he developed some concerns about how we were living. He was especially worried about the amount of time he saw me on my phone and how much time the boys seemed to spend on devices. I didn't like being called out, but I also knew that I needed to welcome his concerns since God was speaking through him to start major changes in our life. And honestly, when I was leaning over David on the side of the road, crying out—screaming—to Jesus to save him, my priorities had shifted big time.

The Boys' Perspective

Our boys felt the roller coaster we were on as well. It was incredibly difficult for these young minds to realize that their dad didn't remember the majority of their childhood. They'd mention a memory, like when we enjoyed a cookout with friends or a particular pet we had or an exciting gift they got for Christmas. David's response was typically a tad aloof or disinterested; he just didn't have context for any of it, and every new memory, even a miniscule one, reminded him of all that he didn't know about our life. The boys acted out more, and we knew they were feeling the same unsettledness. We had some interesting conversations with them about their perspective of it all, such as:

> Me: What was the best part about dad having amnesia?
>
> Evan: It was funny when he thought our dog was just the sweetest thing until he peed on his clothes on the floor! Oh, and one of my favorite moments was when he mooned you! (Cue the laughter of little boys at this memory!)
>
> Caleb: I realized it was a new start. Since I didn't know how long it was going to last, I was preparing my mind for the long run.
>
> Me: What was the worst part about dad having amnesia?
>
> Evan: He didn't do a ton of stuff. He was always tired and didn't really want to do anything except pet the dog.
>
> Reid: He didn't have much energy during that time. He would just lay in bed and look at his phone.
>
> Caleb: I was concerned about how extensive it was—like how far back the memory loss went. When I found out he didn't know anything from like the last ten years, I was really worried. Some

key events happened during that time, and I didn't know what he did or didn't remember. It scared me.

Me: What things did you enjoy telling him or showing him?

Evan: He actually used to surprise us with parts in the movies and now we got to surprise him!

Reid: He could remember most of the original Star Wars movies, but we showed him some of the new ones.

Caleb: We had just gone to the theater to see Avengers: Endgame three days before this all hit. I couldn't believe he didn't remember seeing it, and I tried to tell him about it.

Dealing with the Anxiety

Even though I knew that God was carrying us, I still struggled at times with anxiety and sadness. A week after being home, I wrote in a text to a friend, "It's all hitting me hard today, and I'm tired and just over it all." David couldn't understand all of my anxiety since he didn't even understand our present-day life. I tried to be strong for him, but there were moments when I just wanted out of this twilight zone.

Until you walk through something like this, it's hard to comprehend all the affected layers involved. We are designed to remember for a reason! And when that ability is gone, even temporarily, life can get super hard and complicated real quick.

My parents invited us over for lunch one day and I was grateful to get out of the house for a bit. It was strange to listen to David marvel at the sights on the way that were "new." He didn't remember the remodel my parents had done at their house—and many family members that had joined the family in the past ten or so years were new to him as well. It was such a strange, strange phenomenon. I knew the memories were in there—how could they not be? But for some reason, his brain had them under lock and key. I kept hearing God speak Isaiah 43:18–19 (ESV):

> Remember not the former things, [*WOW!*]
> nor consider the things of old.
> Behold, I am doing a new thing;
> now it springs forth, do you not perceive it?
> I will make a way in the wilderness
> and rivers in the desert.

These verses became a theme for me and gave me hope that I shouldn't get stuck in the memories of the past, but rather listen for what God was doing in the present and for the future.

Sleep sometimes brought me a measure of respite a measure of respite; it was a glorious gift to shut the brain off for several hours and emerge with a fresh outlook for what we were facing. One particular morning, we woke up with happiness and hope, but that state quickly diminished as I became overwhelmed and emotional.

> *I shouldn't get stuck in the memories of the past, but rather listen for what God was doing in the present and for the future.*

David was seeing everything that needed to be done in our house as if it were the first time. (Remember, we were in the middle of a remodel, so our house was a mess!) As he processed all that he saw, he talked about the needs of our house a lot. He would constantly walk around the house and say things like, "That room needs to be painted. Looks like the garden needs weeding. I've got to replace that light. There's another scratch in the floor that needs patching." My personality tends to take those comments as evident failures on my part, like somehow I wasn't good enough—the situation was becoming a recipe for an impending disaster. He also talked incessantly about who we were as a family, where he saw we needed to improve, and where he envisioned us heading. All of those are good things, but it piled on day after day and I could only take so much.

When I finally reached my limit, I started crying; I cried and cried and couldn't seem to stop crying. I had held it together for so long, but I had become weak and was at the end of me. This outburst was a surprise for David; he had no idea that he had been pushing some sort of button.

When we both settled down, God gave us the gift of a very open and raw conversation about our "past" life. It was hard, but good and very healing. He listened to me describe how life worked for us pre-amnesia. We had aha moments as we discovered that we had let life happen to us instead of us stopping to enjoy it; in the process, we had both turned into jerks, building resentment toward life and each other. So much came to the surface in this conversation, and we both felt the love and grace of God being poured out on us as we talked and prayed through it.

A Mini-Miracle

Even though parts of this particular day were extremely difficult, there was also something very special—a miracle happened! Here is the transcript from a video I shared about the miracle that God gave us in the midst of some pretty dark storms:

> Yesterday was a rough day in our world. In the morning, I asked God to give us another memory since David hadn't had a memory from that blocked-out time period surface for a few days. And it's just so encouraging when a random memory comes into his head and we have assurance all the data is still there.
>
> On Sunday, we were driving in the car and listening to music. I realized that David didn't recognize *any* of the current Christian music that was on the radio or that we typically play in church. In fact, when an absolute favorite song of both of us came on the

radio ("Revelation Song"), he negatively commented, "Well I can definitely tell that contemporary music has changed a lot in the past several years." It was very sad because music means so much to our family.

On this morning, we ended up going through a rough patch and a difficult—but good—conversation. Later in the day, we dropped by the church to do something real quick and he said, "We've not prayed today. We need to pray." God is doing some amazing things in our marriage and in our spiritual walk and unity. Amazing. So anyway, I replied, "Yeah, we do need to pray. How about we go sit in the sanctuary?" We went in the sanctuary, sat down, held hands, and just sat in stillness for a while. It was beautiful. We said some special prayers together.

We got back in the car, and I was just waiting for all those memories to flood back in an instant since we had just prayed for that! But God's not going to respond on my timetable or in my way. We rode along, in a place of stillness, headed to pick up some supplies for our chickens.

Then he says, "Hey! Is this a real song, or did I just make it up?" And he starts singing with incredible clarity and beauty the words to the song "Holy Spirit" by Bryan and Katie Torwalt:

> There's nothing worth more, that will ever come close
>
> No thing can compare, You're our living hope
>
> Your Presence, Lord . . .

He sang the entire song with this pure, sweet voice. He knew and sang every word perfectly. I sat in complete awe, knowing that I was witnessing a miracle of God unlocking a piece of David's brain —and he was flooding out this song of praise and worship in the Spirit! The entire song emerged with incredible clarity!

We had not listened to this song in the previous week, not since the amnesia. But we had sung that very song in church on the Sunday when he "crashed" and everything went down.

I said to him, "That's a current-day song!" And in true David-fashion, he was bummed that it wasn't a song he had just made up on the spot. He said, "Man, I would have loved to write that song!"

> I sat in complete awe, knowing that I was witnessing a miracle of God unlocking a piece of David's brain.

We just want to praise God and let everyone know—let the world know—God is still working. God is unlocking memories as He wills. And in the meantime, we are on a crash course of dependence and trust in God's faithfulness and seeing Him come through for us. The Word is alive! Life is alive! We are so blessed today! Thank you for your prayers—it's keeping us going in the midst of what could be considered a pretty devastating nightmare. God is bigger.

A Nightmare AND a Gift

Ten days into this wild ride, David randomly remembered how our family says "scissors!" It's such a small thing, but this little family joke was a special memory to surface. When our youngest son, Evan, was super little and learning to talk, he said "scissors" without the r and with a lot of z's. It sounded like, "sizzizz." We celebrated and smiled big-time when David said it Carroll-family style during a normal conversation.

I didn't understand how this trial could be such a complete nightmare AND an incredible gift at the same time. I wanted to run, scream and hide one moment, and the next, I was thanking God for all that we were going through. I grieved because, even though I had my husband, there was a huge part of him that was gone. I was sad and mad; I wanted him and our life back. There was immense pressure on me to have to know and remember all the things that had to be taken care of. I was also David's resident Google, continually educating him on our life, which took a toll.

Yet it was beautiful at the same time. Our marriage was becoming what I had always prayed it would be. He was becoming the dad that I had always wanted for our kids. We were finally seriously looking at our life and lifestyle and making needed changes. We were being given a season of rest, renewal, and recovery. God was using this story to draw attention to Himself and transform lives all around us. He was strengthening our church members and causing them to rise up. We had a platform for influence and being a light. We were being given a new chance at life, and the Word was more alive in us than it had ever been before.

I didn't want to hyper-spiritualize the experience and not be real. And I didn't want to wallow in misery to the point where there's nothing good show-cased from it all. As I wrote in my journal, "So . . . we feel what we feel, knowing God is a good and understanding Father. And at our core, we have a faith that is unshakeable, even when it's currently being refined in the Refiner's Fire. Thank You, Lord."

David's View of the Time Lapse

Back at home, I wanted to figure out how far back I needed to go to remember life. I got on the internet and started searching for major US events by year. I went far enough back to where I knew that I would remember and went forward from there. I realized that I had missed about ten years' worth of US presidents; I didn't know anything about Barack Obama. It was amazing to see all that had changed in the short span of ten to twelve years. Technology was now everywhere and had captured the attention of the world.

Looking at the past events in this fresh, bird's-eye view was like sitting in history class and learning it all for the first time. In a word, I was shocked at what I was learning. I could see a direct, plotted agenda being laid out for this country. There was so much growing hate and division. I watched the different paths and saw Satan's hand at work. It reminded me of 2 Timothy 3:1–5 (ESV), which says:

> But understand this, that in the last days there will come times of difficulty. For people will be lovers of self, lovers of money, proud, arrogant, abusive, disobedient to their parents, ungrateful, unholy, heartless, unappeasable, slanderous, without self-control, brutal, not loving good, treacherous, reckless, swollen with conceit, lovers of pleasure rather than lovers of God, having the appearance of godliness, but denying its power. Avoid such people.

We don't have to look far to see this agenda played out. People have become proud and divided, lovers of self, and lovers of money. There's division at every turn: government, communities, race, families, and churches. Hatred is growing and it's all part of the world's plan.

It also makes me think of 2 Timothy 4:3–4 (ESV):

> For the time is coming when people will not endure sound teaching, but having itching ears they will accumulate for themselves teachers to suit their own passions, and will turn away from listening to the truth and wander off into myths.

As I looked back over the progression in our world and in churches, I saw some things more clearly than ever before. The ways of the world have penetrated the church. Some churches don't even open the Word of God or mention Jesus Christ. It's more like a country club. And since when do churches need to vote on things that are already established in God's Word? One

> God is sifting the shallow and sharpening the faithful.

way to describe what I saw is that God is sifting the shallow and sharpening the faithful.

One thing is for sure, the world was quickly changing; it was speeding by while I was stuck and sidelined. I didn't know what to do with all of this new information. What I did know was that it was overwhelming to take in, and I was easily exhausted.

The struggle for me was to understand where I fit in with all of this new reality. Was this my existence from here forward, or would my memories ever come back? The more I tried to make sense of everything, the harder it became to do so. I remember trying to explain it to Shannon, "My brain is always tired and full. I'm really trying to live normally, but there are still huge gaps in daily life."

I began to wrestle with the thought of returning to my position as the pastor of a congregation. I tried to talk with Shannon about it, and I know that she was scared at any thought of leaving the church. In my mind, though, I didn't see how I could return to a place where everyone knew me and I didn't know anyone. I was supposed to have a relationship with all of these people, but it had been stripped away. I couldn't begin to grasp how that dynamic would work. Yes, I was told I was a pastor, but I had zero context for what that meant. The thought of going back to the same church made me extremely uncomfortable. What made sense to me at the time was to try and make the most of this situation and go to a different church or into a different line of work. This would not be an easy decision, nor a decision to be made quickly. I saw the outpouring of love from our church, but had no idea how the overall situation would end.

I needed and wanted to work through all of these thoughts, but I was tired and had to rest. I say "rest" in jest, for even in sleep my mind was at work. One night, I had a third vivid dream. In this dream, I was in another long hallway, but this time with only one door at the end of the hall. As I approached and opened the door, there was another door not far inside that would slam. I would then open the next door, and yet another door would slam. That was the dream: one door would slam after each door was opened.

I knew that my mind was trying to sort everything out, but it continued to be frustrating when no answers came.

All of it—the dreams with no answers, the exhaustion, and the frustration—summed up my current status. I came to a crossroads; I could either wallow in self-pity or give it to God. Did I truly believe all that I knew about God? Were His promises true? Did I have faith? The answer was, "Yes!" And it was time to walk in it. I had a lightbulb moment; God was trying to get my attention, and He sure did. I realized that I could not fix this, but God could use it however He saw fit. I had to change my thinking. I had to surrender all of it. I told Shannon that, even though I didn't understand it, I didn't need to understand it. God could use it to help us realize the changes that we needed to make in our lives as well as set new priorities going forward. It might seem strange to hear, but amnesia was actually a gift.

> I realized that I could not fix this, but God could use it however He saw fit.

What's odd to me is that David and I didn't really process our deepest emotions and thoughts together very often *during* the amnesia season. In fact, it wasn't until we started documenting and sharing our thoughts as we wrote this book that we discovered and understood more of what the other person was going through in the journey. I knew that David was struggling, yet he also seemed so strong. He blew me away with his positive outlook. Here's some of the inspiring things he said when he had no assurance that his memories would ever return:

> *"Honestly, I don't look back and regret all the memories I've 'missed'—because I look around me and see all the blessings I have in the present."*
>
> *"It's ok if I never fully know or remember my past, because I know Who holds my future."*

> "I've been thinking a lot about Job this week. From what you're telling me, it sounds like the enemy tried to take my voice to get me to stop singing and preaching. (David has had worsening vocal issues for a couple of years, which was one of the big stressors in his life.) *Now he's tried to take my memory to get me to stop proclaiming the truth. But I'll say with Job, 'Yet though he slay me, still I will praise Him!'"* (Job 13:15)

> 'Yet though he slay me, still I will praise Him!'

More of the Roller Coaster

During this time when David had amnesia, a family member passed away and we attended the funeral. At the last minute, when we were about to walk out the door to go to the service, David insisted that I change the boys' clothes. I had dressed them in outfits that he would have been OK with only a few weeks prior. But he had reverted ten years on me and wanted them in their Easter-Sunday best. It was stressful and difficult for me—and I reacted.

It had all just kept piling up, these little scenarios that by themselves are not a big deal, but one after the other, day after day, ends up creating a mound of plain 'ol hard. It was hard to have to explain *and justify* every aspect of our life to David seemingly all the time. I felt like I was continually in historian mode with regards to our finances, lifestyle, people, routines, important events, and expectations.

I didn't want to react to him or get selfishly tired of serving him, especially when he was being very sweet and humble and gentle. But the whole experience was demanding more from me than I could humanly give. I was—and am still—in need of a Savior to carry me, pour out grace on me, transform me, and give me strength. Thankfully, our God specializes in these things when I humble myself and allow Him access to work on my heart.

About two weeks into this ordeal, David insisted that we clean out our garage. Apparently, this amnesia season gave him a newfound clarity on our life, and he had no idea why he was giving up HIS garage for a chicken hospital and labor-and-delivery ward! Going through everything in the garage was pretty overwhelming for David since he didn't remember what most things were or where they needed to go. But there are such things as amnesia benefits, since we were able to pitch a lot of stuff that I had wanted to get rid of for a long time! We laughed quite a bit about this; I'm grateful that he was so good natured about it all, even though I know it was wearisome for him.

I'll never again take for granted the convenience of automatically saved passwords, calendar reminders, and automatic emails! They saved us big-time. One morning, David walked into the bedroom and said, "I guess I give the dog his meds on the fifteenth of the month. I just got a calendar reminder about that. Um, can you please tell me where the dog supplies are?"

I remember having to tell David about painful things in our past that he didn't remember, including our stillbirth and later miscarriage. He grieved as if he was going through it for the first time. This is just one example of many that happened in our new, temporary reality.

Daily I experienced:

- Sadness, because it was hard.
- Tears, because someone reached out in some way to show us love.
- Fear of the unknown and the future.
- Heaviness, because of all the pressure and responsibility on me.
- Grief for all that had been lost—not just memories but also normalcy, routines, friendships, and our church.
- Awkwardness as he encountered people he "should" know but, according to amnesia, was meeting for the "first time."
- Joy, because I still had my husband at my side.

- Admiration for his attitude, how he was applying himself, and all he could accomplish.
- Anticipation for what God was going to do in and through all of this experience.
- Peace, because I knew so many were praying for us.

Through it all, God was faithful and good.

REFLECTION PRAYER

Heavenly Father, as I read about this roller-coaster story, I'm reminded of specific times in my life when I've felt the same way. I know what it's like to be overwhelmed by the circumstances in front of me, yet feel helpless about how to fix any of it. Your Word says that You never leave us nor forsake us, and we can be courageous and unafraid because of that truth (see Deut. 31:6). Help me to walk in Your promises today and experience victory, even when life is hard.

3
THE MIRACLE

On the first day of this journey, when David was still in the emergency room and we were newly discovering this "random" amnesia, he asked if we ever got away for vacations. I remember having to answer his question with, "No, we don't get away very often. Last year, you were given four weeks off at church, and we only took two of those vacation weeks. And those two trips were for my business." He remarked with a definiteness of purpose, "We need to get away."

Almost daily after that conversation, he talked about the need for us to get away and take a vacation. It was a pressing, urgent necessity on his heart. He talked about his desire to travel far away from life at home so we could gain more clarity and have a respite from the heaviness of life there.

God blessed us with a trip to Florida through some very generous church members. And I just knew this trip was going to be part of our healing story, based on how intent he was and how strongly he felt about it. I hoped that his memories would come back during the trip, but regardless, I knew that somehow just getting away, resting, and being near the ocean was going to be healing for us.

We packed up and headed south for this healing vacation. We were so excited, anticipating a week to remember! Once we arrived in Florida, things started to fall apart a bit. This account from my journal will shed light into the struggles we encountered:

> This has not been an easy vacation so far. I'm praying God will redeem it.
>
> David's needs and expectations for this trip are to be totally left alone. Basically, he wishes he was by himself—not bothered by the demands, needs, and constant chatter of a wife and two young sons. He's reacted to us multiple times.
>
> He ended up telling me last night he didn't know me—I wasn't the same person he married. That really shocked and pierced me deeply. But I can say I don't know him anymore either, and I sense the distance between us. He said he's not going back to the church when we get home from vacation, but instead is going to get a corporate job . . . He went on to vent and say that the kids are irritating with their constant needs, I cater to the kids versus him, and he's frustrated and ready to go home.
>
> I felt like I was going to die last night. Here we've been given this beautiful gift of a trip—and instead I'm walking through a hellacious nightmare.
>
> I don't understand any of this. The layers of amnesia are absolutely awful. I HATE it. His responses at the beginning were so tender and humble. But the longer we go, the more frustrated he becomes.
>
> I'm scared. I'm exhausted from trying to be strong, from trying to manage his needs, the boys' needs and somehow get mine met as well. I'm worried about our future. I'm confused.
>
> I have nothing . . . but God.

So last night on the beach, with hot tears streaming down my face, I cried out to God. I found a way to praise Him for Who He is—how could I not with this massive ocean display in my face? I'm clinging to Him when I have nothing else to cling to.

The book of Psalms has given me immense comfort during this time. The psalmist is real and raw in detailing the sorrows and woes of life. But then he turns his focus to the Lord. There's hope in redirection.

> There's hope in redirection.

I'm trying. By the grace of God, I'm trying. Praying we can walk through this valley well. Praying the enemy doesn't use it to destroy us. Praying for clarity and truth (God's will) to be revealed. Praying we can survive.

God, please intervene quickly.

Being gifted this trip was an answer to prayer. I knew deep within me that we needed to get away and take time to reflect, talk, be still, and pray. As Shannon mentioned, when we first arrived at our destination, it wasn't an easy time. I was unsettled and desperately wanted to make a plan regarding going forward in life. How could I go back to the church, and how could we, as a family, return to anything like it was before? Shannon and I had some intense conversations, and I could see the concern in her eyes. I knew, from everything she shared with me, of her love for the church and our community. How could we come to a decision that would bring peace to our family? I was wrestling in prayer.

Yes, I did say that I didn't know her anymore. The Shannon who I remembered loved to go on fun Krispy Kreme runs and now she and the family were gluten free! We used to be more spontaneous, and now everything had to be calendared or structured. Our complete way of living was vastly different from what I remembered. I needed to take some time to be alone with God and sort out the thoughts and changes that were "happening" in my life.

The next morning, I got up at 5:15 so that I could see the ocean sunrise. How can something so strong and majestic like the ocean bring so much peace? I could listen to the crashing waves all day, every day. I was grateful to have a few quiet moments before my little world awakened.

After having my quiet time, God opened up the door for David and me to have a good conversation. David was more tender and humble—and I believe he heard me on the fact that this whole thing was hard for me too. I told him how his comments and reactions really hurt me, and he listened to my fears about it all. He said that he understood and would work on his communication. We prayed together.

I knew that I could trust God—and that I did. But my flesh felt very unsettled. I recognized that this whole experience could be a complete overhaul of our entire life—and I wasn't sure that I was ready for such a change.

I journaled my feelings about it all, "God, help me trust when all I want to do is run back to 'safety.' I know my definition of safety is an illusion. Jobs, people, friendships are all temporary. They'll all pass away. They can't fulfill. My only true, eternal, lasting safety is You and Your Word. I know my word this year was 'enough'—that You are truly enough. I had no idea what I'd have to walk through to prune me and learn more fully that You are enough. Taking away my husband's memories?? Identity—career—thoughts of life?? Is that what it takes? O God, Your school is painful. It hurts to the quick. But as I fall, I land in the safety of Your almighty, loving arms."

> I know my definition of safety is an illusion.

As the week went on, our vacation got much better and smoother—more relaxed. We settled into a comfortable routine: listening to each other; being open and considerate of the other's needs; and enjoying the gift of rest, relaxation, and God's beauty all around us. It was a true gift. We relaxed for the first time in a long time.

But on Thursday of that week, while the boys played in the gulf waves, we had a painful conversation about our future. David was leaning more toward leaving his job as pastor and getting another job. I could tell that his decision was largely in part to his total lack of memories and subsequent emotional detachment to our church. I cautioned him to not make a decision (1) without including me and (2) solely on his current reality, influenced by the circumstance of amnesia—because it wasn't the full truth.

I felt trapped. It was like he was forging ahead with no thought of *my* emotional attachments! I was scared, yet I also realized that God *could* be leading us on a new path through this situation and that I needed to be open. Boy, the internal battle was intense. Our conversation was good, in that we both talked calmly and truly heard where each other was coming from, but it didn't leave me with any warm fuzzies for our future.

A couple of hours later, without knowing the struggles that I'd been going through, my mom sent me a verse that she'd read in her quiet time that morning, Exodus 14:13–14 (ESV):

> And Moses said to the people, "Fear not, stand firm, and see the salvation of the Lord, which he will work for you today. For the Egyptians whom you see today, you shall never see again. The Lord will fight for you, and you have only to be silent."

These verses hit me straight in the gut and heart. They spoke a gentle rebuke since I had tried to control the outcome and fight my own battle concerning David's condition. Most moments, I trusted in God, but I had many thoughts of trying to fix everything myself. I believed, but I also had doubts. I surrendered, but I had moments of wanting to control. These verses provided clear direction for what I *was* supposed to do—BE STILL. It gave promised hope that the Lord was at work right then, even though I couldn't see any evidence of how He was working or what He was doing. I also wondered if the promise in the verse of deliverance "today" would be applicable to us.

The whole rest of the day, I was way more settled and at peace. When I'd be tempted to worry or fret or ask David questions (with the goal of reassurance), I'd repeat this verse and immediately find the peace of Christ. That evening, I gave into the temptation to look into the possibility of David being admitted to the Mayo or Cleveland Clinic for amnesia—assuming healing didn't come, even though God had promised it would. I should have had more faith.

I knew that God was telling me to lay everything down. He clearly told me that I was not in control of when David's memories would come back. I couldn't control any part of the entire situation; I had to be in a place of total surrender. He gently reminded me, "When you are being still and totally surrendered, I'll fight for you. I'm at work. I'm fighting even when you can't see it. It might look desperate and bleak. You might not see any hope. But just be still."

The week overall was a blessing, but as our time there was coming to a close, I was beginning to wonder if any healing would come. I thought that maybe "healing," for us, was learning to rest and having the gift of relaxing and enjoying God's creation.

One of the things that I loved to do while we were in Florida was get up before sunrise and just sit on the balcony to read God's Word, pray, and watch the sunrise. I got up on Friday morning and enjoyed yet another amazing display of God's artwork. There was no one around. I closed my eyes and listened to the waves roll in on the beach. I sat in anticipation as the first rays of light broke over the horizon. I watched as the gulls soared over the water and called to each other.

I read from the Bible and spent time in prayer. I again watched the ocean and reflected on what I had read. The sun was now clear in the sky, so I stood up, and when I did, everything immediately went black. You know when you stand up too fast and everything gets dim? That's the only way that I can describe it, but it was much more than that. It was suddenly, with a blink—it wasn't gradual. It was BOOM—vision gone! Total blackness.

I was scared and reached out, held onto the railing in front of me, and stood there for what seemed like an eternity, but I'm sure that it was just a few seconds. I thought, "Now what's happening—am I going to be blind?!" Then, I experienced this intense and absolutely wild tingling sensation that started at the top of my head and rushed through my entire body and then went out my feet.

Immediately, in an instant, everything was back to normal and I could see!

At that moment, I realized that I was thinking about church life. Everything had come back into my mind! My memories had returned!

Shannon and the boys were still in bed, but I ran into the hotel room and shouted, "Shannon! I think my memories are back!"

She said, "Are you kidding me right now?"

I said, "Why would I kid about that? Ask me something!"

She said, "I can't think of anything!" I told her that she wasn't helping very much!

I woke up around 6:45 a.m. and was in bed reading Facebook comments from my post from the night before when David rushed into the room—maybe *stormed* is a better description. I had heard footsteps running outside the door, then he swung the door open. Later, Reid even commented, "I'll never forget his face when he came into the room. It was amazing! His face was all lit up, and his arms were out. His eyes were HUGE." David had a look of sheer bewilderment, panic, urgency on his face. It was unusual and instantly got my attention. He exclaimed, "SHANNON! I think my memories are back!!!"

I was SOBBING as he recounted what had transpired on the balcony just a few minutes before. I was incredibly overwhelmed with this absolute miracle!

He told me to ask him a question. I couldn't think of anything to ask; my mind was totally blank! I finally asked, "Who is Donna Craig?" He answered, "Christy Corum's Mom!"

And then we stood there and cried like babies.

Evan saw David run past him and into the other bedroom. "I was sleeping on the couch, and all I heard was mom crying like a baby. So, I came into the room thinking something was wrong and instead Dad said he had his memory back!"

We cried and we cried and we sat on the bed and we praised God! The boys and I quizzed him on more things until we knew the memories were fully back. He successfully answered random questions like (just to name a few):

"What was the name of our dog that passed away?"

"What kind of gardening method do you use?"

"To what city do we travel to meet with our financial planner?"

"Did you ever preach a sermon series on the book of Jude?"

Just as the memories were all gone in an instant, they were fully back instantaneously—in only a way that God could do. It was a complete miracle that we had witnessed.

He was second-guessing himself, so we went over a lot of memories that he had previously not been able to recall. After a while, he said his brain felt full.

I texted our family and a few friends to let them know our big news, and the celebration began. Friday, May 24, 2019, was officially declared a victory celebration day!!

*A picture of exactly where David stood when
God unlocked all of his memories.*

We left Florida the next day to return home. Boy, did we make some memories on this trip!

That Sunday, we decided to go to our church for the first time since that infamous Sunday when David's amnesia started. We walked in and surprised everyone—it was incredible, such a huge, emotional high for all of us! There were so many tears, hugs, praise hands, claps, and smiles. We were finally home.

There were many times in our twenty-six-day trial that I wasn't sure that we'd ever have that reunification with our church family. Honestly, being separated from them and seeing David's complete emotional detachment from them was one of the hardest and most devastating aspects of the whole thing. It was scary.

I knew that God was asking me to surrender all, even our church. And I had to get to a place of "being still" concerning our church, who was like family. It was hard and very painful. I didn't like it—but I know that God doesn't want any of us to hold onto anything in life too tightly. Anytime that we have an opportunity to evaluate our affections toward a person, group, hobby, or job—it's a healthy thing, because even good things can become idols of our heart.

> *Even good things can become idols of our heart.*

Someone asked me if I remember not remembering. Yes! And it was really weird. My brain didn't know what to do with it all. But if anyone ever asks me if I have lost my mind, I can answer, "Yes! But God found it!"

God literally changed our life during this period. He completely changed our perspective, our outlook, our attitudes.

We asked the boys what life lessons they learned from this journey. Their responses pretty much sum it all up. Evan commented, referencing Romans 8:31 in the process, "There's a verse in the Bible that says,

> What shall we say to these things? If God is for us, who can be against us?"

And Reid summarized (referencing the same chapter in Romans, but speaking of verse 28), "I learned that God is in total control—just like it says in that verse: 'All things work together for good for those who love God.'"

Reflection Prayer

God, I'm reminded that even when I can't see your hand at work, I can know you are still working behind the scenes. I know this is true; I've experienced Your faithfulness in my own life, time and time again. Help me to trust You—even when I don't see it. Forgive me for taking matters into my own hands and attempting to control the outcomes. Forgive me for not believing that You're bigger than whatever I'm facing. Please give me the courage to believe that You will fight my battles for me and the grace to just be still. I praise You that You are still a miracle-working God!

4

WHY ME? WHY NOT?

Life-Changing Lesson 1: Suffering is normal.

No one likes suffering. All through this whole ordeal, I found myself saying, "I didn't sign up for this trial. This was NOT my choice of difficulties." If only there was a multiple-choice option to pick the trials that we were about to go through, right?

But that's not how this life works. In fact, even though it's gloriously beautiful at times, it's also painfully hard. We were actually promised there would be hard times as long as we exist on this fallen earth. John 16:33b (ESV) says:

> In the world you will have tribulation [trouble]. But
> take heart; I have overcome the world.

If you've ever been through something difficult, or you're currently walking through a hard time, you can put a big checkmark next to this Bible verse. Got the t-shirt, God!

When we step back and think rationally, what do we really expect this life to be like? I would assume you are much like us in that, when you look over your life, you find that the painful times were when you grew and matured. I know that when I started working out, my muscles *hurt*. And each time that I'd stretch them to a new level in my exercise program, they'd hurt again. Pain means an opportunity for growth. No pain means weakness. But it's through the pain, through working our way past the weakness, that we finally reach our needed destinations and goals.

> Pain means an opportunity for growth.

Why do we react and resist so strongly when we walk through difficulty? One of the most popular questions we hear when we conduct pastoral counseling is, "Why me?" As a general rule, the human race believes, at some level, that we are each above any suffering or difficulty. But it makes me wonder what we're truly expecting. Deep down we know that the reality is that this world is fallen, sin is present, evil exists, and pain is a growth-motivator. At some point in our journey, we must mature and learn to welcome the trial. Why? Because we know that transformation and deeper faith will be the result!

About halfway through our amnesia season (although we didn't know it was halfway; we were bracing ourselves for the amnesia to be a long-term reality), I shared these real and raw thoughts with a friend:

> Amnesia sucks. There . . . I said it. Today has been a day of grieving and being real about how hard this journey is. I've told God how much I dislike this trial. I've cried. I've gotten irritated. I've been *over it*.
>
> I know that God is with us, refining us, showing us more of Himself and creating

> We can feel the pain and be weary yet praise Him in the same breath.

something new. We trust Him; we are surrendered. But it doesn't mean that this is all a piece of cake. We can feel the pain and be weary yet praise Him in the same breath. It's such a strange place to be . . .

A natural tendency for all of us when we are facing struggles is to question by saying, "Why is this happening to me?" I also wrestled with that question. I couldn't figure out what I had done to deserve this lonely existence. I mean, who ends up with amnesia these days? I wondered, "Why was this the card that I got to draw?" However, I eventually came to the conclusion, "Why NOT me? Am I so privileged that I'm beyond experiencing trials and struggles?" I eventually told Shannon my thoughts, "Even though I don't understand this, I don't need to understand this. If God can use amnesia and my suffering to reach one person, then so be it." I had to remind myself of this often when the temptation to wallow in self-pity would surface.

Our suffering had purpose—your suffering can have a purpose. Now there's different kinds of suffering. Some suffering we bring on ourselves. Then there's also a kind of suffering that actually grows us up in maturity. This is outlined in James 1:2–4 (ESV):

> *Count it all joy, my brothers, when you meet trials of various kinds, for you know that the testing of your faith produces steadfastness. And let steadfastness have its full effect, that you may be perfect and complete, lacking in nothing.*

Whoa! Did you catch that truth? Various trials eventually make us "perfect and complete"—which means mature, whole. Isn't that what we all ultimately want? Well, that means we will go through suffering. There's no other way around it. The verse also talks about being steadfast in the middle of testing—and that more testing produces more steadfastness, or endurance. Our first temptation or inclination when we are hurting is to make it stop or find a way to escape. We aren't born with a natural ability to look forward to long, drawn-out trials. Quite the opposite. Yet, over time, after many difficult and painful experiences, we begin to learn that these varied trials we despise are the very tools that God will use to grow and mature us to look more like Him.

Think for a moment about some of the deepest and most spiritually mature people that you know— or the people that you love being around because they exhibit rays of light and wisdom. If you were to ask them their life stories, they would most likely be wrought with many trials, difficulties, and sorrows. *Suffering is the school for gentleness; suffering produces character in a way nothing else can.*

> Suffering is the school for gentleness; suffering produces character in a way nothing else can.

Check this out from Romans 5:3–4 (ESV):

> But we rejoice in our sufferings, knowing that suffering produces endurance, and endurance produces character, and character produces hope.

Rejoice here can actually be translated to mean "boast"—when was the last time that you boasted or were proud about your suffering?! This conversation has taken a turn, hasn't it?! But we see the progression— embrace your suffering because it increases your faith muscle and eventually you end up with more hope.

We had a choice when David's memories were absent and we were trying to figure out life. And honestly, our responses and attitudes landed on all the ends of the spectrum. Sometimes we moped and complained (mostly me). I questioned and cried out to God and asked for this to be taken away. But somehow, through God's grace, the majority of our attitude was surrendered. Our minds were set, and we saw how God was starting to use this situation to change us and others, and we intentionally chose to embrace it.

We want you to know that it's OK to be real before God, especially when we are hurting. He doesn't want us coming to Him with a religious piety and praying with big, flowery words. In fact, Jesus warns us that He has no interest in Pharisaical, hyped-up prayers.

> And when you pray, do not heap up empty phrases as the Gentiles do, for they think that they will be heard for their many words.
>
> — Matthew 6:7 (ESV)

Rather, we believe He wants us to come just as we are—broken, needy, wounded, angry, tired. He specializes in taking broken messes and transforming them into beautiful messages of His glory. Don't feel pressured to pray perfectly—just like we talk to an earthly friend, He wants to hear our hearts as we pour them out to Him.

> *He specializes in taking broken messes and transforming them into beautiful messages.*

Don't Answer Us Yet!

There were times that I knew everyone was praying for David's memories to be restored, but I knew that it wasn't the right time for God to answer our prayer. We still had more rich lessons to learn, and God wasn't done refining us in the fire. I knew that the memories would return when we were finally at the place that He wanted us, and not a second before. We stood in that place of confidence and surrender, letting God do His perfect work in and through us.

A popular question many ask during a time of suffering is, "Did God *cause* this suffering?" Honestly, we don't know that we can secure the definite answer to this question 100 percent of the time—much more will be revealed about each of our "behind-the-scenes" stories when we get to Heaven. And sometimes, determining the "cause" of our suffering isn't the most important question.

Here's what we do know: We didn't listen to the warning signs that were there for months prior to amnesia; and there is such a thing as cause and effect in life. (Warning: Consequences of not taking care of your mental and emotional health may include amnesia!) It could have been self-induced; it was absolutely God-allowed. He is not always the *cause*, but somehow, He is able to use every single situation for good. We don't know how He does it every time—but He can truly redeem anyone and anything. For us, "this light momentary affliction" was, as 2 Corinthians 4:17 (ESV) says:

> Preparing for us an eternal weight of glory
> beyond all comparison.

And that's part of the secret to learning to suffer well: changing our perspective from just seeing our present-day pain, to focusing mostly on (and looking forward to!) the glory of eternity in Heaven, where there will be no more suffering.

Many friends sent us meaningful gifts while we were suffering with amnesia. One dear friend gifted me the updated devotional book, *Streams in the Desert*. This work will go down as one of my all-time favorite devotional books—as the authors speak about how our faith-walk is deepened primarily through the tool of suffering. This devotional has helped to shape our understanding of suffering and learn to fully embrace it as an absolutely necessary component of our Christian faith.

A God Who Can Temporarily Remove the Senses

As one of our friends pointed out, God has a history of taking away senses of those in the Bible to get their attention! This idea was fascinating; we had never thought of it before. In Luke 1, Zacharias, the father of John the Baptist, is rendered mute for his wife's entire pregnancy because he did not immediately believe the promise of God about his son (see verse 20). As soon as his son was born and Zacharias obeyed God, his voice was given back. His first words were of praise to God (see verses 63–64). We're sure that he had a lot of time to think during those nine months of stillness. God used that time of his being mute to get his attention.

The Apostle Paul was blinded for three days after his conversion (see Acts 9:8–9). He had been going one direction, attempting to persecute those who followed Christ. After God got his attention and he was converted, he had some in-depth heart-work to do before he would be commissioned to be the greatest missionary that ever lived. God had to take away his sense of sight to do a deep dive on his heart.

We felt this same way. God had removed the memories for a time to drastically get our attention. We figured out pretty quickly, it was in our best interest to comply and surrender our hearts, especially since we had zero control on the return timeline of his memories.

Praise You in this Storm

I'll never forget David saying one night, "No matter what—though He slay me, yet will I praise Him" (see Job 13:15). His faith was solid, and he inspired me to praise through this storm.

This is one of the major keys of suffering, although it feels incredibly counter-intuitive. It completely changes our anxiety levels and focus when we can praise God *while* we are walking through hardship. Why is this so powerful? We believe there are two reasons. First, praising God gets our mind off of ourselves and our little circumstances. When we focus on the storm, it's no surprise that we become afraid and overcome with grief or anxiety. Praise so gently turns our eyes away from the storm and onto the One who

We have to choose to turn our head and heart away from the crashing waves and onto the calming Way-Maker.

calms storms. This reality reminds me of one of my favorite choruses: "Turn your eyes upon Jesus, look full in His wonderful face. And the things of earth will grow strangely dim, in the Light of His glory and grace." We have to choose to turn our head and heart away from the crashing waves and onto the calming Way-Maker.

Secondly, praise reminds us who is in charge. All of the sudden, when we praise, we can picture God Almighty, seated on His heavenly throne, overseeing all the world. We realize, as David so often says when he's preaching, "He's not pacing the floor or breaking a sweat over this issue. He's God." He can handle whatever the situation is. When we are reminded of His character, we find peace. We remember that He is a mountain-mover and that our mountain is not too big for Him.

There are times when I am so broken and empty that I cannot physically praise. I just don't have the words and my heart is too heavy. In these times, I will do one of two things. I like to open up the Psalms and read them out loud as my prayer. The Psalms offer much comfort as the writers are real and raw and pour out their hearts to the Lord. They always include praise as part of their prayer, and when I read these words from Psalms out loud as my own prayer, it somehow lifts my spirits and gives me renewed hope.

The other thing that I do is turn on praise music. Sometimes it's a specific song and other times, it's a radio channel or app that plays praise and worship music. Listening to music during times of suffering is a powerful exercise. It lifts our soul, refocuses our mind, and helps to bring peace.

I remember both of the nights that David was in the hospital and I went to my parent's house to spend the night. All of these scary realizations of what we were facing were new and raw, and I had many questions. I was flooded with grief and feelings of being overwhelmed. Both nights, I played specific worship songs that friends sent me as an encouragement. As I laid in bed in the dark and listened

> We would praise scared.

to the words, I lifted my hands and praised. Trust me, it wasn't easy! I had tears streaming down my face and my heart was torn and bruised. I had experienced trauma, and I had no idea when we'd get healing or resolution. But those moments were special. They became the foundation of who I would be and how I would respond during this entire trial. We would *praise scared*.

Another way God uses suffering is to impact other people, which is why we decided to live this story out loud. At first, we started posting on social media as a way to answer all the questions of friends and family and keep them in the loop. Many people had lots of questions about this strange phenomenon; they couldn't wrap their own brains around the fact that their friend, David, had such a severe amnesia; I needed one platform to give a single update where everyone could see it. But very quickly we saw this story was gaining the attention of a lot of people. And we intentionally decided to post and share openly *while we were going through* the trial.

Many of us don't get to experience a real-time trial of another person very often. We usually only hear the grandiose story after the last chapter has been written. Living out loud when we didn't have an answer was hard. We had doubts. I often thought, "What if this goes on for four—six—eight months and we still don't have a miracle? Will people think I'm foolish or lose interest in our story? What if God doesn't come through like we've said He will?" We had never before let people into our heart or struggles or faith-journey so intimately. In fact, David had always been a fairly private person and not in favor of me posting many personal things online. Vulnerability was not something that was comfortable for us. But it was powerful and healing—for us and for others.

Obviously, you don't want to blast every negative experience on social media or drown your friends in your constant stream of woes. That's not the spirit that we are talking about here. Use common sense! But just know that when you decide to live out loud for God in the midst of every situation—even the painful ones, others are strengthened in their own faith as they watch how you respond to your trials.

Most people do a really good job of wearing the "I've-got-it-all-together" mask, while inside, they are broken and falling apart. One of the things I have often said to the church is, "We are a group of people that are all just one big, hot mess." We need to stop pretending, especially in the church, and start being real and transparent with the people that God has placed around us.

There is such a thing as learning how to suffer well. We know that sounds crazy, but it's true. Since suffering is inevitable for all of us, we can either fight it and become bitter and weak, or we can learn how to respond to it with humility and openness. You probably haven't been through a month of severe amnesia. But we bet you've experienced disappointments, financial struggles, health fears, wayward children, strained relationships, or childhood trauma. We are so sorry for your pain, and part of us wishes that we could take it away. But we also know that, if you will surrender to it, even learn to boast in it, pray like you've never prayed, and praise through the storm—you'll come out the other side a stronger person, one who is way more equipped to make a difference in this world.

> There is such a thing as learning how to suffer well.

We want you to know that, no matter what you're walking through right now, you are not alone. There is a God who has promised that "he will not leave you or forsake you" (see Deut. 31:8 ESV). It might feel like the world is crashing down around you and you can't find your breath. You may believe that all hope is lost and that there's no way forward. Those feelings are real; we acknowledge your pain. Yet we are here to cheer you on with this voice of truth—in Jesus, there is hope in each moment of every day. He is the "friend who sticks closer than a brother" (see Prov. 18:24 ESV), and He actually cares for every single thing you are facing. All that we are asking is that you make one choice to turn to Him, talk to Him, let Him hold you.

We also encourage you to find someone you can talk to; going inward isn't healthy. Learning to suffer well means allowing safe friends or counselors into your broken space, even when you're hurting. None of us were made to go through life alone.

A song that comes to my mind often when I'm hurting is "Friend of a Wounded Heart" by Wayne Watson. Maybe it will encourage you too:

> Smile, make 'em think you're happy
> Lie and say that things are fine
> And hide that empty longing that you feel
> Don't ever show it, just keep your heart concealed
> Why are the days so lonely?
> I wonder where, where can a heart go free
> And who will dry the tears that no one's seen?
> There must be someone to share your silent dreams
> Caught like a leaf in the wind
> Lookin' for a friend, where can you turn?
> Whisper the words of a prayer and you'll find Him there
> Arms open wide, love in His eyes
> Jesus, He meets you where you are
> Jesus, He heals your secret scars
> All the love you're longing for
> Is Jesus, the friend of a wounded heart

Your suffering has purpose; your life has meaning—and nothing is wasted in God's economy. We gently challenge you to change your perspective, check your thoughts and mindset about your pain, and just look for God in the middle of your suffering. He's there—arms open wide, love in His eyes.

> Your suffering has purpose; your life has meaning—and nothing is wasted in God's economy.

REFLECTION PRAYER

Oh God, this is hard. I'm reminded of my pain and all the hurts right now, and thinking about turning it all over to You scares me. But I desire to praise You in this storm—even though it means I have to "praise scared." Help me learn how to suffer well and grow to look more like You. You're going to have to pour out a lot of grace on me as I commit to changing how I've looked at and responded to this suffering. I need You, Father!

5
PUTTING IT ALL ON THE TABLE

Life-Changing Lesson 2: God doesn't want us to live a stress-filled life.

Another by-product of this amnesia experience was that it caused us to do surgery on our life as we knew it. Yes, it hurt. Big-time. But there was no way that we could go through this time and *not* change the way we lived. If ever we got a sign from above, this was it and life in the Carroll household would never be the same. Here's the awesome message for you too—you don't have to go through a month of amnesia in order to learn some of these life-changing lessons. We will walk you through *why* we changed our thinking, *how* we changed it, and *what* the results were. We think that you'll be inspired to "do some surgery" and get it all out on the table as well.

Whether I liked it or not, David was in critical-evaluation mode while he didn't have his memories. To be honest, it was exhausting and a lot to take in at times. We are typically open in our communication and constantly evaluate our life together. But this state of evaluation was a whole new level! He had fresh eyes on our life, a brain that was totally clear, and a desire to not repeat damaging patterns.

We all have lots of stuff—and if we're honest, we really do like all of our "stuff." We had to put all of our stuff on the table—the chickens, garden, house projects, careers, and lifestyle. We decided to get rid of a lot of it—the things that aren't important and aren't going to matter in eternity. Philippians 3:13–14 (ESV) says:

> *Brothers, I do not consider that I have made it my own. But one thing I do: forgetting what lies behind and straining forward to what lies ahead, I press on toward the goal for the prize of the upward call of God in Christ Jesus.*

When we read God's Word, it should force us to evaluate everything. We live in the richest country in the world and have so much stuff that's not going to matter one bit in eternity. Stepping back from our day-to-day life, we can start to see how we live for material things most of the time; our stuff controls us, to a degree.

When we truly see that God is in control of it all, it should cause us all to stop and listen for God's direction. Sometimes it comes down to the things that we do, like our hobbies. There's nothing wrong with a good hobby. But maybe God is saying, "I want you to do away with that good thing so that I can do something awesome in your life." Sometimes we get so invested in the things and in the stuff that we miss what God is trying to do and say and how He is trying to lead. This was where we were pre-amnesia.

David had a complete emotional detachment from the things he didn't remember. Talk about a fascinating study—to discover how attached our memories are to our emotions! It was strange to hear him talk about something that he had previously been passionate about (and maybe even called to), yet because he didn't remember that hobby or interest, he was completely disinterested in it.

Evaluating Everything and Decreasing Stress

We really did start taking a deep dive on everything and every aspect of our life as we knew it. David couldn't understand why we lived on a large homestead with chickens, a massive organic garden, an orchard, a pond, a tractor, etc. While he had amnesia, we argued back and forth about developing this homestead and making it a priority. He kept saying, "It's too much!" And I replied, "But we had decided that it was super important to us to have this homestead and be self-sufficient. We had even dreamed of living off-the-grid someday. It's one of our *values*. In fact, I named my Instagram handle '@carrollhomestead'!" (It's now been changed.) To which he rebutted, "What's Instagram?!" Ugh . . .

Our identity had become wrapped up in our stuff. We had mistaken our values for our identity. We had given ourselves too broad of a scope of all the things that we considered to be important. All of those things were *good things*. Yet they were wearing us out, and David was able to discern that with his new perspective.

> We had mistaken our values for our identity.

When I told him about our church life, he couldn't understand why he would simultaneously take on the roles of worship pastor and senior pastor. I remember telling him about his church responsibilities while we were in the hospital. David shook his head and quietly commented, "It's too much. Why did I ever let all this happen?"

He was starting to see that the doctors were most likely correct in their assumption that the amnesia was precipitated by cumulative, unaddressed stress. It was either the brain shuts down or explodes. As a protective mechanism, the brain literally locked down years of stress and refused to give David access to those memories—the good ones *and* the stressful ones.

Stress is a killer—and sometimes a rather silent killer too. Why then do we either wear it as a badge of honor or ignore it as if it isn't a real threat? We know that stress is a risk factor for heart disease and stroke. And now we know that it's also a risk factor for losing your mind. This was a monumental lesson for us and caused us to make major shifts in how we were living and thinking in order to not fall into the stressed-out trap again.

New Pathways

For me, another interesting and somewhat difficult process during amnesia was finding the balance between being his historian and allowing him to be open to creating new pathways for life. Let me explain. As his twenty-four seven Google, I became an expert of recounting the past. But I didn't just tell him about the factual circumstances, I found myself explaining to him *how he had felt* (or how *I perceived* he had felt!) about things that we had gone through.

A small example of this aspect is when he expressed deep concern and shock over our lifestyle. He questioned me, "Why in the world do we have these things?" I didn't just tell him that it was his idea, but I would start to explain how he used to *feel* about those things. I'd say things like, "You loved having these hobbies. You poured yourself into our homestead. You had a value of being self-sufficient on the land and being able to create so much goodness from scratch. You even helped a baby chicken hatch in your hands and found such purpose in life on this property."

But I started to notice that how he previously felt about parts of our life didn't match his present feelings. There was a disconnect. Part of me wanted to belabor the point of how much he loved our previous life—because I was grasping for some type of grounding; I was longing to go back to our "normal."

I remember one day the Lord prompting me to not focus as much on telling (or maybe even persuading) him about his previous emotions. That effort was limiting. God was wanting to do something *new* in our lives and, if I kept being the *emotional* historian, I could possibly stop this new path forward. I needed to give David the facts, but then let him decide how he felt about it *in the present*. This allowed him to have clarity and discernment, and it eventually led to our ability to make some major life changes.

Once again, these verses, from Isaiah 43:18–19a (ESV), came to us:

> Remember not the former things,
> nor consider the things of old.
> Behold, I am doing a new thing;
> now it springs forth, do you not perceive it?

We believe that there are seasons when God is wanting to move us forward, to do something new in and through us. The danger is getting stuck in our old ways, saying, "that's how we always did it," and limiting the possibilities of what could be. Learning from the past is valuable; staying stuck there is destructive—and it can halt our minds and hearts from seeing this new vision that God is wanting to bring to pass.

Looking back over the years, we were near burnout or breakdown multiple times. We had been through countless conversations together about life being too busy and full and needing to get rid of something. We had put homeschooling, church life, homesteading, my home-based businesses, etc. on the table over and over again. But nothing significant ever came off the list. Instead, we continued to push forward, taking on more and more (instead of less and less), which we now realize was simply insane! And, eventually, that insane approach led to amnesia.

Your Turn

The gift of amnesia was David's ability to emotionally detach from life and make totally rational, unbiased decisions with a clear mind. If you are sensing that burnout from too much stress is impending—or you're just tired of the general rat-race pace of life, here are some suggestions we would offer to you:

- Pretend (as best you can) to be an outsider looking at your life. What do you see? Or ask an actual outsider to give feedback on your life. Then, listen with an open mind to their insight. (Over the years, our family had commented multiple times that we were too busy and stressed, but we didn't pay attention. Shame on us!)
- Make a list of everything (big and small) that currently demands your time and attention. Put each item on a sticky note and literally place them all on the table. Pray over them. Rearrange them. Consider each one, and ask the questions listed below.
- Ask really hard questions and answer honestly—even if it's painful.
    - What is the greatest source of stress in my life right now?
    - Will this activity or aspect matter in one year, five years, ten years, or when I die?
    - If I picture or imagine getting rid of _____, do I mostly feel sadness or relief?
    - What are the people closest to me frequently saying about _____?
    - What is my gut saying to me?
    - What do I most want to be known for?
    - What do I want my kids to remember about these years?
    - Do I know my purpose in life? How does this _____ move me forward with my purpose?
- Include a trusted friend on this whole process to hold you accountable to making tough decisions.

- Pray, pray, pray about God's *best* for you in *this season*, then be still and *listen* to His voice and leading. He loves answering this prayer from His children who are seeking His will in every situation.

This exercise is not a one-and-done activity. Rather, this is something that we will need to revisit over and over, in each season or chapter of our lives. There are shifts in our interests and values over time. For example, I am eternally grateful for the season that we had homesteading. I loved learning to can vegetables, hatching and raising chickens, going four-wheeling in the back field, and seeing the boys fishing in the afternoon. It was a beautiful season that will provide life-long, pleasant memories. But it wasn't a forever season for our family. We had to be open to changing and pivoting with the changing season.

Another example of this lesson is that I loved serving on multiple teams and in various capacities within our church. But I saw, through all of the amnesia experience, that I was doing too much, and it was taking time and energy away from my primary priorities. I removed myself from some church responsibilities as I got laser-focused on what mattered most in this season. The enemy of the *best* is often the *good*.

> The enemy of the best is often the good.

Intentional Living

David and I, who both have strong drive and vision, had to give ourselves permission to just be still. In fact, we discovered that part of our identity had been rooted in being busy, productive, and constantly providing value to others. Rest wasn't accepted in our pre-amnesia world. We didn't value vacations and time away like we should have. There was always a to-do list, a vision or project to tackle, or a garden to weed.

As we made these hard decisions, we had to be extremely intentional. We had to remember our why: to simplify, destress, and learn to enjoy life more as a family.

Shortly after David's memories returned, we started in earnest to prepare our house to be put on the market. It was emotionally painful to put our gorgeous homestead up for sale, but it was also imperative in our quest to simplify. We started to put family and just-us getaways on the calendar and actually make them a priority. We started turning our to-do lists over and choosing to take an afternoon nap. We spent more time just being together, running errands together, and filling our time with what filled our souls.

Even though we now had freedom and the green light to make some big lifestyle changes, it wasn't at all easy to do. Here are some thoughts I expressed about two weeks after his memories had returned:

> It's one thing to say that we are changing our life and lifestyle after such a dramatic and traumatic experience like what we've recently walked through . . . it's another thing to actually *change*.
>
> I'm learning that if I'm going to change my lifestyle, I first have to change my *thoughts*. Ouch! It's my thought patterns that determine my behavior —not the other way around. This realization is where the hard work begins (in the mind), where true transformation takes place.

It's my thought patterns that determine my behavior.

> This week has been challenging for a number of reasons. But one particular reason is I've come face to face with the thoughts (lies!) that are toxic and have contributed to the way that I've lived.
>
> Anyone else have an "inner critic"? Guess what?! This inner voice lies! It tells me that I'm not good enough, so I have to behave in x-y-z way in order to win approval. It keeps me in fear of being

my true self, because I'm afraid of what others would think if they saw the real me. It holds me back from potential, change, and transformation by whispering lies. It keeps me in stress and busy mode, never resting.

I've come face to face with some of those lies this week—and it's been painful. But we are committed to true and lasting change because of all we've been through. The war is on! Change is worth it . . .

You see, we act or behave a certain way because we first *think* a certain way. If you're interested and ready to discover a new way of living, you're going to have to first be willing to battle your thoughts. We will warn you that it's not going to be easy. Your thought patterns have built up over time to develop habits that have turned into your present-day to-do list and schedule. This is going to require some soul-work to emerge with different habits.

Brain Breakthrough

The brain works in mysterious ways, so many of which are unseen, unknown. A vast array of neurons are buzzing and churning, providing life and essence to our body—though "out of sight, out of mind" for most of us in our day-to-day routines. It's not until a portion of the brain's activity is on lockdown that we even notice all it's capable of or how it serves us daily.

My background is as a registered nurse. I worked in the Emergency Room, Cardiac Rehab, Employee Health, Management and Community Outreach departments for many years. I loved learning about how the body functions and how it all fits together. Yet I took for granted the role of the brain and how we must attend to it and

When was the last time you did self-inventory on your brain health?

support our own brain health. When was the last time you did self-inventory on your brain health? We take quizzes on our heart health, diabetes risk, weight, sleep, etc. But the brain is vastly overlooked.

Our brain is our most-needed organ. It's the command center for the rest of our bodily functions. One of our favorite teachers on the brain is Dr. Caroline Leaf, who instructs with a fascinating belief that the brain has the ability to heal itself and can be controlled by our mind. We highly recommend any of her books. In fact, during David's time of amnesia, he poured himself into her book *Switch On Your Brain: The Key to Peak Happiness, Thinking, and Health*.

Days after David's diagnosis, we started researching brain health as if our life depended on it. I couldn't believe that we had missed these truths and warning signals from his brain for so long.

I put together a Brain Breakthrough protocol for David, and he implemented it religiously during his amnesia battle. Several of these practices are still an important part of our daily regimen now, as we work to continue to protect our brains and allow them to function optimally. David's brain had such clarity during those twenty-six days. Part of that detail is due to years of stress and memories being locked away. I believe that the brain was healing and recovering during this reset. I also think that these measures we took to support his brain health contributed to his clarity. (It's also interesting that his clarity a year after the event is still quite intact! The experience itself changed him; the supplements he's still taking support his brain, and the lifestyle changes that we've instituted are paying off.)

Here's our Brain Breakthrough protocol. For a more detailed version, please visit our website at www.DavidAndShannonCarroll.com.

- **SLEEP**

    The brain resets itself and heals when we sleep. We must work to get eight hours of solid sleep as adults, yet this is an area where many of us fail miserably. It is not something to be proud of when we say we only need or get a few hours of sleep each night! Your brain is suffering if you aren't giving it adequate time to rest, process all the information it took in during the day, and reset.

David spent a lot of time sleeping during amnesia. And honestly, he had huge sleep needs even after his memories came back. He was overwhelmed with remembering all of life before amnesia, remembering all that happened during amnesia, and then having his memories return and needing to put all the pieces back together. His brain got full very quickly after the memories returned, and the best coping mechanism was sleep.

To this day, we prioritize sleep. When we are tired, we go to bed. We retire early and often get up early—but if we need to sleep in, we allow our bodies that privilege. David often takes about a thirty-minute nap in the afternoons when he gets home from work, just to give his brain a break. I used to nag him about sleeping (confession time), but now I let him sleep when he feels the need to do so. It's one way that his brain is telling him to stop and slow down.

We use essential oils to help us sleep soundly. Some of our favorite sleepy-time oils are: cedarwood, lavender, and chamomile.

- **VITAMIN B**

    A quick web search will help confirm the great importance of supplementing with all the B vitamins, if brain health and memory support are some of your wellness goals. David experienced greater clarity and mental energy with large doses of vitamin B.

- **OMEGA FATTY ACIDS**

    We decided to have a steady diet of mackerel or salmon in order to get consistent intake of omega-3s. It is well known that these omegas are essential for cognitive health and might even help with mild memory loss. David took the highest daily dose of OmegaGize3, which also includes vitamin D3 and CoQ10.

- **NUTRITION**

  We often think about our nutrition affecting our waistline and heart. But when was the last time you ate for your brain? This was a new concept for us as well. But after doing our research, we implemented the following nutritional tips into our lifestyle:

  - Decrease sugar intake! (This is huge. And beware! Sugar is in everything. It's incredibly damaging to our body and brain.)
  - Eat more raw nuts. We kept a bowl on the counter of raw almonds, walnuts and pecans, so we'd all be more likely to grab a handful whenever we had the munchies.
  - Increase raw fruits and vegetables, especially berries and green vegetables. Not only do these foods provide essential vitamins our body needs, they might also improve the brain's ability to create new neural pathways, which was a huge goal of ours!
  - We already discussed the value of omega-3 fatty acids, found in salmon or mackerel or tuna. We made sure to eat one of these fish at least once a week.
  - Add antioxidants! We can only get antioxidants from a diet rich in raw fruits and vegetables, and most likely, relatively few of us as Americans are getting enough intake to counter the effect of free radicals in our environment.

- **CHANGING OUR THOUGHT PATTERNS**

  This "natural" treatment didn't cost us any money, but it's probably the hardest change to implement. We realized that our thought patterns needed to be rewired, and we had been given a gift of a reset to accomplish those changes. We recommend Dr. Caroline Leaf's 21-Day Brain Detox Plan as part of her *Switch On Your Brain* content.

- We intentionally worked to "take captive every thought" (see 2 Cor. 10:5 ESV) and evaluate if each thought was productive or damaging. Our thoughts have such power over our brains! We've got to be better gatekeepers of the thoughts that we allow to linger inside.

- Negative thoughts or words were not allowed. (More on this topic in chapter 6!)

- We became quick to forgive or make things right if there was an offense.

- We learned to praise and hope through the storm instead of worry or become anxious.

- We played Scripture and music often as a way to get truth into our minds.

- We worked to get to the root of why we fell into the trap of extreme busyness and stress.

In this chapter, we've filled a toolbox of resources and tips you can adopt to help "save the brain" and have your own brain breakthrough. Our brains were not meant to take on enormous amounts of negativity, stress, sugar and processed foods, or lack of sleep. As the command center for our entire body, the brain deserves a little more respect. We believe that many cognitive deficiencies can be prevented if we will work to implement these tips in this chapter. Will you join us on a quest to "save the brain"?

For more information and resources, please stop by and visit us on the wellness page at www.DavidAndShannonCarroll.com.

Pretend that You Have Amnesia

A truth that we have learned through this experience is this: "What keeps you from changing for the better is you." Let that sink in. We allow our minds to be consumed with what we think that we need, based on what we think that we are supposed to be or what others think that we're supposed to be. When is the last time you stopped to think and ask yourself, "What truly brings me joy? What excites me? What makes my heart sing?" It's so easy to get stuck in going through the motions of life that we actually miss life itself.

> What keeps you from changing for the better is you.

This is your moment to pretend as if you have amnesia. I wouldn't wish the actual experience on anyone, but maybe a few pretend-amnesia moments will help you get more clarity on your life. Imagine forgetting everything that currently fills your day to day living. You have a totally clean slate in front of you, and you get to decide what fills your days and how you will live. Will anything be taken off the table? Maybe some of the things that have been nudging your heart will make it onto the table. It's totally your call—let amnesia work for you in this moment as you decide, and then pursue, what matters most.

REFLECTION PRAYER

Heavenly Father, thank You for caring so much about me and my life. Thank You for doing something new, for breaking the chains of my past hurts and sins and pouring out Your Spirit on me. Thank You for giving me life abundant and making a way for me to walk in total freedom. I commit my life to You and Your purposes; I want my life to count for what truly matters! I ask Your Spirit to reveal areas where I need to do some housecleaning. Please show me clearly the things that I need to get rid of because they aren't the best that You have for me in this season. And give me grace to obey you with everything in me, so my life can bring You much glory.

6
A CLEAN SLATE

Life-Changing Lesson 3:
It is possible to have a reset in your relationships and live with a clean slate.

Inside one of the most difficult aspects of amnesia was also one of the greatest blessings. (Isn't that often the case when God is at work?) Our marriage wasn't bad pre-amnesia, but it definitely has taken on a whole new level of intimacy and joy post-amnesia. Several people have asked us, "How can I have better relationships without having to go through amnesia myself?" We hope to answer that question for you in this chapter.

Speak Life

While we were in the hospital during those first few days with amnesia, we had the opportunity for a couple of fun and special conversations about our marriage, as David worked to "get to know us" all over again. I'll never forget David laying in that hospital bed with me sitting beside him, holding his hand, and after a calm period of silence, he sheepishly looked at me and asked, "Can I ask you a question?"

I replied, "Sure!"

He quietly asked, "Do we, um . . . like, you know . . . make love . . . you know . . . often?"

I laughed out loud—this was not the question that I was expecting. After I answered him, he got this huge, almost embarrassed smile. Truly—*everything was new* to him in our relationship. What he knew of me and us was what he remembered from our years of dating and early marriage. He had so many questions, and I can't even imagine how unsettling that perspective was for him.

One evening in the hospital, David was quite overwhelmed with this whole new reality. We were both grieving over all that was missing in his brain; it was heavy, and we had no context for how to handle any of it. He was humble and vulnerable; he cried often. During one of those moments, he looked at me with tears running down his cheeks, "I just don't know who I am. You say I'm a pastor, but I don't know what that means. I don't know how to be a pastor. I don't know what kind of husband or dad I was. I'm just so lost."

To see this powerful man incredibly broken was almost too much for me. He had no basis for his identity—no ego whatsoever. I had the absolute privilege of speaking life over him and telling him who he really was. With all the love I could muster and tears running down my own cheeks, I moved to his side, grabbed his hands,

> I had the absolute privilege of speaking life over him and telling him who he really was.

and said, "David, when we first got married, I'll be honest with you—I thought of myself as the spiritual leader in our home. But over the years, you have run so far past me. You are an incredible man of God that I look up to, that I learn from, that I honor. God's hand is all over your life and ministry, and I have the greatest respect for you."

This kind of talk was not normal for me (but he didn't know that!); I had previously failed at praising and affirming my husband. Oh, I was an expert at telling him the things that I didn't like or approve of. But as I spoke words of life and breath into his brain and soul, we both just sat and cried. It was a magical moment, one in which I realized how much power my words have over my husband! Truly, it is as Proverbs 18:21 (ESV) says:

> Death and life are in the power of the tongue,
> and those who love it will eat its fruits.

I committed at that moment to intentionally speak more life over him, to help shape his newly discovered identity with affirmation and praise. I am not always successful with this and fail often, but I'm grateful for growth and God's grace on this journey.

Nothing Negative

We all loved recounting stories for David and watching his response to the narrative of our lives. Often, after a few stories in a row, David would end up raising his hands and saying, "I can't take any more stories. My brain is full." And then we would have to keep our mouths shut for a while and not share any new information. Looking back, it's ironic to see how excited we were to tell him all the stories of our life—knowing that he actually experienced them in real life too—yet he had no present recollection of them. Strange for sure.

Anyway, I distinctly remember being in our bedroom, and I was sharing with him stories of things that had happened over the years with our boys. I filled him in on some very tragic and traumatic circumstances. It was a whole lot for him to absorb, but at the moment, I was just rambling on and on with the difficult stories and seasons and details of our past. He paused, looked at me and clearly said, "Shannon, I don't want to know ANYTHING negative anymore about anyone in our past—EVER. Please don't share any negative information about anyone in our life again. I don't have context for anything you're sharing, and my brain doesn't know where to put all of this new and troubling information. If there's something important that I need to know, I'll figure it out. Otherwise, I don't want to know."

> *I remember as Shannon was telling me these difficult stories from our past, I felt physically ill. It was so overwhelming and everything inside of me was emphatically wanting to reject what I was hearing. I understand that some information is necessary and useful. However, in this situation, I did not want anyone's reported history to determine what I thought about them or how I interacted with them. The Bible says that we will be known by our fruit, and I wanted to give everyone an opportunity to stand on their own merit.*
>
> *I was at a place where my mind could not reconcile negative information. I would hear something difficult or painful and it literally would just swirl around in my brain. I had no context for knowing what to do with the stories I was hearing, and I couldn't figure out what to do with it all. It was information overload with random puzzle pieces that somehow were all mixed up and put in the wrong box.*

> I wanted to give everyone an opportunity to stand on their own merit.

I was totally shocked and blown away by his stance. And he stayed true to it all throughout the twenty-six days with amnesia (and beyond). I'm ashamed to admit how many times I had to bite my tongue and stop myself from sharing negative information. I had no clue how natural and normal it was for me to dwell on and talk about the negative. I found myself wanting to share historical events about people in the church, confidential counseling situations that we had led with friends and church members, poor choices that our boys or other family members had made, personality quirks of others that irritated me, etc.

David's stance on this issue was shocking to me, and it caused me to respect him even more. I was in awe of the fact that he could so clearly define and communicate this desire to speak life because he knew and sensed in his spirit the dangers of gossip. With basically a clean slate in his brain, he experienced how damaging it was to add in negative layers of information. He desired to keep his mind clear of those things that would weigh him down.

Amnesia and Marriage

One day, David came up behind me and touched me unexpectedly. In my startled state, I remember reacting, "I have taught you for twelve years that I don't like to be tickled like that! Don't make me reteach you all of it in five minutes!" We laugh about that incident now, but it's just an example of the millions of little details that were completely missing in his mind. Thankfully, he's a quick learner!

This amnesia season had negative and positive effects on our marriage. Some days were plain hard; as you've already read, the layers and layers of this significant of a degree of amnesia were complicated and difficult.

We all take for granted how our collective memories over the years with a spouse form our relationships. Over time, we develop patterns and traditions together. Our memories and conversations shape how we treat each other. We create certain relationship codes of conduct. How we act and talk toward each other now is the result of years' worth of experiences together.

> *Basically, you wake up one day and all you have are your vows— but you realize that there is much missing.*

Imagine all of that being gone. Basically, you wake up one day and all you have are your vows—but you realize that there is much missing. Wow. That scenario was the one that we found ourselves in, and it was extremely hard and distressing.

It was also a challenge for me to see the "today" reality yet still remember our traditions, nuisances, growth points, and inside jokes. So much felt lost. Sometimes I would look at him, when he didn't remember who I had become, and recall in my mind several of our shared memories from over the years. Then I'd realize in that moment that he didn't have a clue that those specific memories had ever existed. I felt alone, and I prayed this during one of those times of grieving:

> It's only Your grace, God, that can turn these painful and tragic circumstances into a beautiful new start and a clean slate in our relationship. I'm hurting and realizing how much is gone right now . . . Thank You, Father, for Your grace when we fail in our human responses. Our faith and our marriage is strong, and this trial will prove only to strengthen it further. But, dear God, please restore and redeem this quickly!

Let's talk some more about what this clean slate actually meant and how it drastically changed our marriage. Early on, I realized that this season could actually provide a positive contribution to our marriage, if we let it.

We had and have an incredible and wonderful marriage; we've been best friends from the beginning. But I hadn't comprehended how much everyday, cumulative stress affected our interactions. Pre-amnesia, there was occasional irritation in our voices when we'd have a "discussion." (OK, let's be honest—we'd yell at each other sometimes and tempers would flare!) Memories of past hurts had led to some guardedness. Normal, broken stuff that we all work through . . .

During amnesia, though, David consistently treated me beautifully. Because any memories of hard times or stressors were gone—there was a new and surprising easiness to our communication, a tenderness. Did you hear that? He didn't remember that we had an argument the night before amnesia, what each other's hot-button hurts were, or times when we had not shown each other grace. And when he didn't have any memories of hurts (so there was a totally clean slate and complete healing and forgiveness in his heart), the way he interacted with me was *different*.

David couldn't control the memories being gone, so his reactions were a normal by-product of the amnesia plus an intentional decision of his to respond in love. I *did* have the memories . . . I remembered the hurtful things that we both had said during our argument just a couple of days prior (no wonder he had experienced chest pains); I remembered the stressful interactions and times when we got on each other's last nerve—and I had a choice. I could continue to react out of brokenness, or I could make a conscious choice to embrace this new, clean slate. And if we're honest, we all have that opportunity to choose forgiveness —even without a diagnosis of amnesia.

> *And if we're honest, we all have that opportunity to choose forgiveness — even without a diagnosis of amnesia.*

Life is too short to hold grudges and relive or rehash past irritations! Let our story be an inspiration to keep short accounts, reconcile quickly, and live in true, God-honoring love with each other. It's totally worth it! And when I saw the beauty that was available on the other side of letting go, I wanted it. I wanted it more than I wanted to hold on to grudges and keep letting the stress-pile add up.

Both David and I are strong, driven, type-A personalities. When we are flying in sync, we are a dynamic duo. But when one of us is irritated, frustrated, or feels like we're threatened or not in control, we can turn from dynamic to dynamite: BOOM! Learning the marriage dance of putting the other's needs before our own has been, at times, a struggle. We've had to try really hard to communicate better over the years. And we definitely grew big-time in our first twelve years of marriage.

But what we noticed is that when life got tough—when stress increased, when finances got tight, when sickness hit, when deadlines loomed, when the kids were overly needy, when house or car stuff fell apart, when we were just worn out—we'd take it out on the other person. Why do we do this? Why is it so easy to tear down the people we love the most—especially when we know that they aren't the problem? This destructive tendency was a pattern in our lives.

Even with the knowledge that his memories were gone and the stress of amnesia in general, David was incredibly relaxed and peaceful. Especially early on, there was never irritation or frustration in his voice. In fact, the first time in this whole trial where he totally lost it and had a complete "meltdown" was when I served a quinoa dish for supper. When he saw the dish sitting on the stove, he said, "Ewww! I hate this stuff and, no matter what you try to convince me of otherwise, I promise I NEVER liked it before either! I refuse to eat it, and I'm tired of all these changes around here. I'm going to get a burger!" And I've not served quinoa since then.

With every memory of our disagreements, stressors, hurts and disappointments now absent from his brain, he had so much room for love. We became very quick to ask forgiveness or *quickly* say we were sorry if we hurt or offended each other. We started to assume the best intentions in one another and spoke life and affirmation over each other—often. We had our finger on the pulse of the relationship at all times and worked intentionally to keep the household a place of peace. Here's something that I learned: true, deep forgiveness (with a measure of forgetfulness) is life-changing. We were given a clean slate in our relationship—as there always should have been.

> *True, deep forgiveness (with a measure of forgetfulness) is life-changing.*

Amnesia for Everyone

Imagine being able to put every negative thought out of your mind. Now, we might not be able to remove every single negative thought, but we absolutely do have a choice of what we hold on to. It would benefit everyone to have a little more "amnesia"—willingness to let go of anything that we carry due to spite or pride.

There are some amazing thoughts from Scripture about what God chooses to not remember.

> I, I am He who blots out your transgressions for my own sake,
> and I will not remember your sins.
> — Isaiah 43:25 (ESV)

> For I will be merciful toward their iniquities,
> and I will remember their sins no more.
> — Hebrews 8:12 (ESV)

What we see from the above two verses is a profound forgiveness from an amazing God. The fact that the God of the universe knows everything, yet is willing to choose to forget my egregious sins is truly remarkable. If He can have a little selective "amnesia," then I think that we can too.

It's also interesting to think about what we, as believers in Christ, are commanded to remember, according to Scripture. Memory is important—God designed for us to remember—and it's a common theme throughout Scripture. We are to remember:

- The Sabbath Day – Exodus 20:8
- The blessings of the Lord – Psalm 103:2
- The gift of God through His Son, Jesus Christ – John 3:16
- The example of heroes in the faith – 1 Corinthians 11:2
- The sacrifice of Christ on the cross, through the act of communion – 1 Corinthians 11:24
- The deeds of God – Psalm 77:11
- All that God has brought us through – Psalm 143:5

As you can see, there are definite pros and cons to amnesia—in Scripture there are instances that we are to remember and instances that we are to follow God's example and forget. Most of the time, we tend to flip these scenarios around and remember or focus on the sins in ours or others' lives and forget the goodness of God. We challenge you to switch your thinking to match God's when it comes to forgetting and remembering.

A Clean Slate Is Possible for All of Us

We believe that the lesson for all of us is that we are all given an opportunity to forgive. You can choose to let go of past hurts in your marriage, disappointments from those you loved the most, betrayals, and stressors. Or you can choose to hang on to them and keep your relationships strained. It's your choice.

> We are all given an opportunity to forgive.

Obviously, there are some sins done to us that we definitely *need* to remember. If you are in an abusive or toxic relationship, that is not OK and you should never overlook that kind of situation. Please get help! You deserve to be safe.

For the majority of us in the majority of our safe relationships, we need to learn how to keep a much shorter list of offenses. We need more amnesia in our relationships. Proverbs 19:11 says:

> Good sense makes one slow to anger, and it is
> his glory to overlook an offense.

Overlook an offense? That's kind of radical in our culture, isn't it? Who does that? I'll tell you who does it: people who desire peace and unity, people who think of the needs of others over their own, and people who are compelled by love.

Everything in life boils down to choices. When you think about your relationships, family, church, jobs, or dreams—the current status of each one of those things is based on the choices you make and have made. It's time to become self-aware and take ownership of your life, specifically the choices you've made. For example, how you think about and respond to others is a choice. Consider the ultimate benefit of releasing a past hurt—or the eventual detriment if you decide to hold onto it. Be honest with yourself, and consider this question—if your marriage could be stronger, if your relationships could be better and you knew exactly how to make them that way, would you be willing to make the choices needed to accomplish that increase?

I'll let you in on a secret: The ability to achieve better relationships in all aspects of your life is already resident within you. Philippians 2:3 (ESV) says:

> *Do nothing from selfish ambition or conceit, but in*
> *humility count others more significant than yourselves.*

In other words, choose to see the goodness in others. Choose to understand others' perspectives. Choose to listen. Choose to forgive. Choose to love.

The most profound example in acquiring a clean slate is what Jesus did for us—in spite of us.

> *But God shows his love for us in that while*
> *we were yet sinners, Christ died for us.*
> *— Romans 5:8 (ESV)*

All of the hurts, disappointments, and bitterness that you might have experienced in your life can be redeemed through the blood of Christ. Making the choice to lay all of your past and sins at the feet of Jesus is the first step in acquiring a clean slate. Here's the reality: The Bible tells us clearly that all have sinned and fall short of the glory of God (see Rom. 3:23). We're all in the same boat, and we are in need of a Savior. All of humanity is offered the free gift of salvation through Jesus Christ. Romans 10:9 (ESV) tells us:

> *Because, if you confess with your mouth that Jesus is Lord and believe in your heart that God raised him from the dead, you will be saved.*

It goes on to promise in Romans 10:13 (ESV):

> *For everyone who calls on the name of the Lord, will be saved.*

You can come into a relationship with Jesus Christ right now, at this very moment, and it is the single most important choice that you will ever make in your life. He is ready and waiting to give you a clean slate for eternity.

You, me, your spouse, friend, co-worker, and children are all equally broken, and when we look at each other through that lens, we can begin to see each other through eyes of grace. You, too, can have a clean slate—without having to lose your mind!

Reflection Prayer

Wow, God! I'm feeling a little overwhelmed right now with the potential for freedom and this clean slate in my own life and in my relationships. I definitely long for this renewed state and am seeking with all my heart for cleansing. Show me my next steps—where I need more amnesia in my relationships and where I need less. Help me see others the way that You see them and learn to overlook an offense. Thank You for the gift of salvation through Your Son, Jesus Christ! Thank You that You have saved me, cleansed me, accepted me, and forgiven me completely.

7
THE NEED FOR COMMUNITY

Life-Changing Lesson 4: Community is a gift from God.

Very early on, it became clear one of the main characters in our story was the Church. Mostly this included our local body, where David was the pastor and had been employed for thirteen years, but it also extended to include believers and a community of friends from all over the world. How they ministered to us, and how we ministered to them, during this season was so powerful and important that we decided to devote a whole chapter on the Church in this book.

You might not be a part of a local body of believers, but you can still glean some nuggets from this chapter. For one, you'll see how Christians are *supposed* to treat each other! We had a front-row seat to experiencing some of the most unbelievable love and service that you've ever seen. This amazing show of community is how we are to live and be known.

But another reason for including this chapter is that the topic of our church was quite a trigger for us. The fact that David had no recollection of his place of employment, the only church his kids had ever known, and the birthplace of hundreds of our special memories was almost impossible for me to wrap my brain around. His brain had successfully locked down any recollection of our church life. It was inexplicable, and it demonstrated to us that pastoring had taken more of a toll on him than any of us had realized.

His lack of emotional attachment to our church, combined with my *very* deep emotional connection to the people and memories, was a huge source of strain for us. It was like we were playing tug of war—continually. It was exhausting and hard; I'm sure that you've already picked up on that particular struggle as our story has played out throughout this book.

I'll never forget the evening when a couple of church friends came over to our house. It was one of the first times that David was officially "meeting" people. It was refreshing for me to be around them, knowing that they were part of my present-day life and we had shared memories of life together. But it was emotionally exhausting for David.

I found out later that Shannon had prompted our friends to walk in, shake my hand, and introduce themselves as if it were truly the first time we were meeting. All in all, getting together went well, and they were very gracious and kind. However, the entire time that we were together, I couldn't help but think, "It is so strange to know we've had a long-standing relationship with this couple, and I don't remember them at all." I was extremely grateful for their understanding, but, at the same time, it was an emotional overload. This scenario played itself out a few times during the twenty-six days, and I found a way to insert humor by joking, "Each time meeting you is like the first time!" It was my attempt to help make everyone feel more comfortable and not so serious.

We started a beautiful routine of writing letters to our church that were to be read during the service each Sunday. I had to smile each time that we wrote and sent a letter; it reminded me of the Apostle Paul writing the New Testament letters to encourage and exhort the friends that he had met on his journeys. It was special to be able to share these personalized interactions with our dear friends. We'd love for you to imagine yourself sitting in our church congregation, knowing what you know about us and our story so far, and hearing these words read from your absent but engaged pastor's family—in the midst of their trial:

Dear Church Family,

We wish we could be worshiping together with you all this morning. The events of this week have been completely unexpected and rather bizarre.

All memories from our church family, current life, and home are temporarily gone. This is super devastating and hard for all of us to comprehend. I wish I could snap my fingers and bring back all the memories and moments and friendships we've shared as a church. In time, it will return . . .

We are spending our time resting, seeking the Lord, researching, and tending to our family. We are choosing to see the positive and give God much glory through our suffering. David said yesterday, "I'm not worried about knowing my past, because I know who holds my future." We have cried and questioned—but our faith in God is stronger than ever. We sense His peace, and we know He is up to something amazing. Only God could take a nightmare and suffering such as this and redeem it for all of our good!

We have been overwhelmed with the love and support from our church family. Even though David doesn't currently "know" any of you—what he does know is we are surrounded by people who love and give fiercely and sacrificially. You have ministered to us and been the hands and feet of Christ. There aren't enough "thank-yous" in the world to communicate our gratitude.

Please continue to pray for us! Obviously, we are praying for David's full memory to be restored in time. But more than that, we know God has our attention and we want to be still and listen and then be obedient. Pray for our boys; it's hard when your dad doesn't readily remember important moments in your childhood. Pray for those stepping in to lead and continue God's work at Vienna Baptist Church. Pray that others will come to know Jesus Christ through our story!

I wish I could give you all a hug right now. We trust that God is working all things together for all of our good . . . and what does "all" mean? (Side note: This is an inside joke with our church because David often says, "All means 'all,' that's all all means.")

We love you and look forward to seeing and "meeting" you soon.

Blessings and Love,
Shannon and David

After our church heard this letter during the service, they gathered around each other and prayed for us. *This* is why we need community and were designed to do life together—the support we can offer each other during times of suffering is one of the best gifts that we can give.

I was quite shocked when the next week rolled around and David wanted to pen the words to another letter to the church—a community of strangers to him in that moment:

Grace and peace to you in the name of our Lord Jesus Christ. I have no words that can truly express the joy and hope you have brought to me and Shannon during this time. Your meals, cards, and words of kindness mean so much, and I sincerely thank you.

We've all been given the guarantee of walking through trials in this life, but it's how we respond to these trials that matters. I know that I have not arrived at complete spiritual maturity (James 1:2-4 ESV) as I still get frustrated and tired. However, what I do know is that God is in control, and I am honored to be used by Him no matter in what way He chooses.

Walking this path has caused Shannon and me to really take a long, hard look at how we were living life. We are praying about what is really important. It is so easy to get sucked into the comfortable ways of this world and stop listening for God's leading. We get on the crazy cycle of busyness, which then leads to survival mode, rather than actually living life to the full.

Even though my memories of the last decade, and then some, have been locked away, I will tell you what really matters. While it would be wonderful to regain those memories, I look forward to what is ahead. I echo the words of Paul that the most important thing in this life is the Gospel of Jesus Christ and Him crucified. The things of the earth will fade and pass away, but Christ Jesus is forever.

Please be encouraged as we all press on toward the prize, knowing the promises of Christ are true and we are all still in this race together.

I truly look forward to being with you again. My love is with you all in our Lord.

Pastor David

Pastoral Burnout

Since all memories specifically from the church were completely blocked, we can assume there was some pastoral burnout going on that precipitated the brain's shutting down. We obviously didn't realize it until it was too late—but now we are way more passionate about it and want to bring awareness to this widespread issue. We hope that you'll consider your pastor or leader as you read this section—and pray about how you can bless them today.

Ministry is incredibly rewarding and fulfilling. Where else do you get a front row seat to watching God literally change lives? There's nothing else like it. We love serving within our local body.

But ministry is also extremely difficult. Pastors are on call twenty-four seven and deeply feel the weight and responsibility for the welfare of others. We hurt with those who hurt and rejoice with those who rejoice. We are the natural go-to when someone is suffering. We give and pour out continually. We war in prayer for others. We preach and wonder if it's making any difference. We sacrifice in order to serve and be present with others. We are at the church all the time. We are a part of countless confidential situations and conversations.

It might look like we are sailing through life on the outside, but inside, many of us are burdened, torn, tired, and stressed. I think that one of the biggest dangers in churches is when people assume that the pastor is OK because "he looks fine." We have to "look fine" because the needs of others are so great. We have to be there for everyone else, and it's an honor to do so. Unfortunately, there is not always a consistent person to be there for us. And if we aren't careful in creating healthy boundaries, we can easily pour out more than we receive. Burnout happens in ministry more than most realize.

Obviously, a pastor has to definitely be called to endure the demands of ministry. For many of us, the calling outweighs the difficulties. Yet we don't want to overlook the difficulties of pastoring. It's time to bring attention to this silent suffering and call the church to action to adequately provide for and minister to their earthly shepherds.

If you are blessed and privileged to attend a local church, here are some things you can do to serve your pastor and help ward off burnout:

- *Pray diligently for your pastor and their family. Those in ministry often have a big target on their backs and walk through a lot of tough situations.*
- *Frequently tell your pastor specifically how their sermon, prayers, visit, or life-example helped you. Send a card or tell them about the specific ways that they've impacted you.*
- *Get involved in a small group or Bible study or Sunday School. Develop relationships with others in your church—partly so they can help surround you when you go through hard times (instead of solely leaning on your pastor when you are struggling).*
- *If your need or question isn't urgent, wait to call your pastor until their posted office hours.*
- *Don't expect their family to be perfect. They aren't!*
- *Ask your pastor how they're doing, and then listen. Ask how you can pray for them.*
- *Send your pastor and their family a gift card to enjoy a date night or time away from the church.*
- *Consider, as a church, paying for a counselor or mentor for your pastor. Just having a safe place outside of the church to vent and be discipled would be a huge gift.*
- *Offer your pastor an occasional sabbatical for a time of refreshing and refocus.*

The Final Letter

As we wrote the final letter to the church *together*, we were getting weary in the ongoing trial. We didn't know that we'd be worshiping with this community the very next week, with David's memories of each of these friends fully restored. These words captured the simultaneous tension and hope we were facing:

Dear Precious Church Family,

What a blessed Lord's Day this is! Honestly, any day the Bride of Christ gathers to worship, fellowship, and look toward the Savior is a good day.

David and I want to continue to thank you all for truly surrounding us and showering us with love, prayers, meals, and cards. It is so special to receive each card and picture you all are sending as a way to reintroduce yourselves to him. This is such a loving and patient gesture by our church family. Thank you. And yes, I stand and cry as he opens and reads each one. You all mean so much to me. (Sidenote: The members of the church started sending us cards in the mail with pictures of their families, interesting information about them, and special memories they had with David. It was beautiful.)

It's only been three weeks since we've entered into this trial, but it feels like an eternity. We want to exhort all of you about extended suffering. Trust me—we all want the easy button and the quick way out of anything painful and unpleasant. None of us likes walking through the fire. We're all looking for the detour or the time capsule to catapult us to the peaceful end-destination.

But that's not God's way. He tells us in His Word we will experience trials and troubles. We will walk through the fire. We will be pruned. We will be crushed on the Potter's Wheel. And is God absent during these painful times? Not at all! The same God who was with the three men in the furnace has promised to walk with us through (not around) the valley. Isaiah 43:2 has comforted us:

> *When you pass through the waters,*
> *I will be with you;*
> *and through the rivers,*
> *they shall not overwhelm you.*
> *When you walk through the fire,*
> *you shall not be burned;*
> *And the flame shall not consume you.*

So what do we do when the suffering seems to go on and on? It's very simple. We dig deeper. We cling tighter. We hold fast to His Word, to continual prayer, and to each other. That's what we are doing, and that's what we encourage you to do as well. Let's make the most of this trial in our Body—for our good and His glory.

We know several of you are suffering right now as well. Your names and specific concerns are present on our hearts, and we are lifting you up to the Father.

I don't know when we will be back to fellowship with you. The church council has graciously given us a time of rest and renewal, which is such a gift. Thank you for understanding and being patient. Right now we are focusing on relearning our own life and seeking God for next steps. David has slowly "met" some of you as he is able. Pray for our reunification as a Body soon.

We love you all—more than you know. And we long to see you— here, there, or in the air!

In Christ,
Shannon and David

I'm sure that you can imagine the smiles on everyone's faces when we surprised our church the next Sunday by showing up for the service—memories and all! Talk about a celebration! We had walked through a lot of pain and uncertainty together, and we watched a miracle of restoration and redemption play out before our very eyes. The unity and faith of the entire community was strengthened. David briefly addressed our friends on our first Sunday back and said, *"It's so good to see you all . . . and actually know who you are!"*

The Body of Christ is called to pray, and the community we are in did just that. Then they took their prayers and turned them into action. It was difficult for us to receive so much love—it's

> Then they took their prayers and turned them into action.

way more comfortable for us to be on the giving end than the receiving end. But we saw that love is a powerful healer; when people are reaching out to show love in all sorts of ways, it helps to heal our broken hearts as we're suffering.

God prompted people to come and pray in our front yard. Someone would send me a link to a song on YouTube as a way to encourage me. A friend would drop a hot meal on our front porch. We had told everyone that we couldn't talk to them when they brought food because it was too overwhelming and difficult for David to see people that he didn't know. So, they'd put a meal on the front porch, ring the doorbell, and leave and we'd go out in a minute to collect it. Then, as I opened these delicious meals, I'd just stand in my kitchen and sob. It was difficult to understand that someone loved me so much that they would spend their day cooking for my family in our time of need.

And this is why God designed for us to live in community. We're not meant to ever be a Christian in isolation—ever! We're designed to be in a family, to weep with those who weep and rejoice with those who rejoice. And when it works, it's beautiful. And life-changing.

> *So then, as we have opportunity, let us do good to everyone,*
> *and especially to those who are of the household of faith.*
> *— Galatians 6:10 (ESV)*

When times of intense trials happen in a local church body, it opens the door to one of two possibilities. On one hand, the people of the church can become scared and react from a place of fear, which can lead to a place of destruction. I have known some local bodies to split and, in some cases, close altogether after a crisis.

But there is also another possibility, the possibility for the people of the church to react in a Christlike way that makes the church even stronger. The latter is exactly what happened in our church. The community was truly sharing each other's burdens, they were coming together in prayer, they were reaching out in love, and—most importantly—they were seeking Christ for every response. When a church body is united and of the same mind, the Holy Spirit is able to work through each person to encourage one another and glorify God.

How to Serve Others When They're Hurting

One of the gifts of humanity is being able to serve and help others. There is something within each one of us that wants to make a difference in another's life. But, if you're like us, sometimes you just don't know what to do or how to do it. We often get stuck in analysis paralysis and then end up doing nothing.

> There is something within each one of us that wants to make a difference in another's life.

Here are some of the actions people took to serve us, without being asked. Something that was a key blessing for us was not even being asked what we needed, because it was hard for us to know how to answer that question. When people said, "What do you need?" I wanted to honestly reply (scream) with, "You could start by bringing my husband's memories back!" I didn't know what to say, which is why some of the biggest blessings were when people stepped in without being told how to.

When someone is hurting or suffering, you can:

- Take food over to them. It doesn't have to be fancy or even homemade. Pick up a pizza, get carry out, or fix a simple meal. Set up a meal train online. Some of our family even sent groceries to us so our pantry would be stocked. (And this was a true labor of love since we are poultry-, gluten-, and chocolate-free in our home!)

- Give a gift card to a restaurant. Even better—stick it in a card and send it through the mail.

- Send a text message that just says, "I'm thinking about you today. No need to respond." Relieve them of the need to respond to you and you'll be giving them a huge gift. Giving with no expectation of a return is the right spirit.
- Send a YouTube link to a song that speaks to you in tough times.
- Send some "happy mail." We received special, inspirational books, Scripture cards, essential oil rollers, funny cards, and "just thinking of you" notes in the mail.
- Sweep in and take their kiddos away for a bit. Bonus if you also pick up their laundry to do at your house!
- Gather friends together to pray for the person who is struggling.
- Mow their grass, clean their house, or take their dog on a walk.
- Share jokes and funny stories with them to help lighten their spirits.
- Offer to take them out for a meal or drive, but respect it if they need space.

Any action that you take out of a heart of love will be well received. You see, love in and of itself *is* a powerful, healing force. Somehow love received comes in and washes over broken hearts. It smooths rough patches. It offers hope when you thought that all was lost. It reminds us that we aren't alone, and it meets our most basic need for connection and value. Learn to love well.

Learn to love well.

First Corinthians 13 is a familiar passage that is often read at weddings, but it's actually a mandate for how the *Church* is to act. As you read some of these verses, we encourage you to do some self-reflection. Replace your name or your church's name with the word "love." Is this how people would describe your character and actions?

[Insert your name or church's name here] is patient.

[Name] is kind and is not jealous;

[Name] does not brag and is not arrogant,

[Name] doesn't act unbecomingly;

[Name] does not seek its own,

is not provoked,

does not take into account a wrong suffered,

does not rejoice in unrighteousness, but rejoices with the truth;

bears all things, believes all things, hopes all things, endures all things.

[Name] never fails.

How did you do? How does your church or community group measure up to this description? We propose to you that if more churches and Christians were marked by true love, the world would look like a much different place. We desperately need each other, and honestly, we aren't sure how some make it through difficult trials without a strong community to surround, pray for, and help carry them. Let's be a people that heal the world through our love.

Reflection Prayer

Heavenly Father, thank You so much for Your design for community—it's beautiful and I see how You created us to need each other and walk through life together. Forgive me for times when I've been so self-absorbed that I've not loved others well, especially when they were hurting. Please prompt me when You want me to serve in a specific way and help me be obedient. Show me how You want me to encourage my pastor as well. I want to be Your hands and feet, making a practical and real difference in the lives of those You've put in my circle. Thank You for Your love—I want to be a conduit of this kind of love to the world.

8
ONE THING REMAINS

Life-Changing Lesson 5:
God's Word prevails and remains.

The last lesson we want to share with you is about God's Word and how, even in spite of all we went through and all that was lost, God's Word remained. Hebrews 4:12 (ESV) is our theme verse for this life-changing lesson, and it reads:

> *For the word of God is living and active, sharper than any two-edged sword, piercing to the division of soul and spirit, of joints and marrow, and discerning the thoughts and intentions of the heart.*

Even though my memories were gone, we discovered that God's Word surpasses even that kind of circumstance! His Word is implanted inside of us, somewhere deep within. "I have stored up your word in my heart, that I might not sin against you" (Ps. 119:11 ESV). His Word was still very present, even when so much else was missing.

Honestly, the thought of God's Word remaining, even when David's memories didn't, is the most prevailing lesson for me through all of this experience. Early on in our amnesia journey, I was praying out loud with David and I quoted a verse in my prayer. After we finished praying, David lovingly corrected, "You know, that's not how that verse goes . . ."

In typical Shannon-fashion, I retorted with, "Yes, it is."

He laughed, "No, it's not."

After continuing the banter a few more times, I gave in and Googled it . . . and realized that he was right. (I hate it when that happens!)

In that moment, I saw that the Word of God was still very fresh in David's mind. Even though he didn't remember our home, our dog, our friends, or even where we banked, he remembered everything he had studied about the Word of God!

In some ways, David's personality and perspective had reverted to ten-ish years earlier. His understanding of culture and current events, his jokes, his frame of reference, and his thoughts about life were from many, many years prior. It was strange to witness. It was like he had been transported in a time capsule from 2009 to 2019.

> In that moment, I saw that the Word of God was still very fresh in David's mind.

(This is the stuff movies are made of—it was *that strange!*) It's like taking someone who doesn't get out much to a party; somehow what they're saying just doesn't fit with the context of everyone else in the room.

David tried so hard to fit in quickly and get up to speed on current events, but he still had regressed in many ways in his understanding and context of the world and our life. He felt this gap very acutely, and it was painful and embarrassing for him. I hated seeing him struggle, and I tried hard to fill in the missing pieces. I became proficient at whispering quietly to get him up to speed in a conversation. He became an expert at just rolling along with whatever was going on and then asking me about it later. Or, at times, we just broke the awkwardness in the conversation and made an amnesia joke.

We had to "introduce" him to family members that had joined the family since his last memory. I just can't imagine going through life and 95 percent of the information coming into the brain is *new information*. It's overwhelming, yet that's what David experienced, and we adjusted as best we could, also adjusting our expectations of David being "the old David."

David had zero memory of preparing sermons or preaching sermons. Zero. He was shocked to learn that he was a pastor of a thriving church and had been for ten-plus years, eight of which he was in ministry full time. He was the expert on anything related to our church building, activities, and people. Pre-amnesia, I was constantly amazed at how knowledgeable he was about every little detail of church life. Obviously, his calling was this body of believers, and it became his life.

A few days after coming home from the hospital, he brought his Bible home from the church and would frequently flip through it. "Oh, it looks like I did a sermon series on James at one point," he would muse. There was no recollection of any of the *actions* that had been second nature to him. No matter how many times we took him to familiar settings, like his church office, or even played back sermons that he had preached, he could not remember any of it. Forty-plus-hour ministry work weeks for the past eight years were just gone.

It was on the way to Florida when he finally agreed to listen to one of his recorded sermons. This willingness was a big deal, since the thought of doing so had previously been too overwhelming for him to even consider. Just imagine that your current identity—based on your career, lifestyle, and hobbies—all being gone, and all that you know is what you observe and what people tell you. We didn't get through the whole sermon; after a while, it was too much for him and I had to turn it off. But what we noticed is—it still gives me goosebumps to think about—earlier that very morning, he had said some of the exact same phrases and concepts that we later heard him repeat in that recorded sermon!

He didn't remember the countless hours of study that he had spent in the Word of God. *But the content and evidence of transformation was obvious and present-day!* He didn't remember the actions, but he was still living out the *fruit* of God's Word in his life. Are you catching this? This reality is huge! Personality was ten-years regressed. *But character and knowledge of God's Word were PRESENT-DAY DAVID!* We witnessed signs of David's spiritual investment over and over and over again during those twenty-six days.

> But the content and evidence of transformation was obvious and present-day!

David had grown immensely in the Word and in his character as a man of God over the previous eight to thirteen years—and even though every tiny detail of memory from those years was gone, he was still the *same David* in the areas that mattered most. This truth brought me such comfort and peace. It was like an anchor and reminder that everything was going to be okay. Trivial, fleeting information was gone—but his soul was intact, and that soul was feeding his mind and behaviors in a positive way.

And it taught me the most valuable lesson of all: Somehow, someway, the Word of God lodges in a part of our brain or body that is separate from just our memories. Maybe a better description is that the Word of God lands *deeper* than our mind, to a place that cannot be damaged or taken away. I saw firsthand how *alive* God's Word is, how it transcends thought and lives in our soul. Remember Hebrews 4:12, which says that the Word of God is "piercing to the division of soul and spirit, of joints and marrow" (ESV). It's hidden deep within a part of us that is spiritual.

> Somehow, someway, the Word of God lodges in a part of our brain or body that is separate from just our memories.

Amnesia can steal memories from the mind, but it can't touch the part of us that is eternal!

David didn't remember the act of reading or the actual content of several other non-Bible books or TV shows or movies. As I mentioned earlier, he had no understanding of current music that he had once loved. His context definitely illustrated that every memory of those other media experiences was gone—nothing was left from those.

> *Amnesia can steal memories from the mind, but it can't touch the part of us that is eternal!*

But it was different with the Word of God, because the Bible is no ordinary book. It is truly "living and active" (Heb. 4:12 ESV)!

Any time that we spend in the Word of God is worth it. When we are *hiding God's Word in our heart*, we are literally doing something that has eternal value. We are allowing it to touch a portion of our soul and spirit in a supernatural way. When the Bible says to be "transformed by the renewal of your mind" (see Rom. 12:1–2 ESV), it means it. The pages of Scripture somehow have a way of transforming a part of us that we can't see or touch. No time in God's Word is ever wasted.

This proved to me again that God is real as I saw this wild, real-life demonstration of how spiritual and natural were vastly different and only one thing truly remained. I witnessed in front of my own eyes this unexpected, new evidence of God's existence and power.

> *Only one thing truly remained.*

If you have a Bible but haven't read it in a while, get it out and wipe the dust off of it now. It alone has the power to redirect your life and help you discover who you really are. Its truth transcends memories and even life itself; it's eternal.

This fact should encourage all of us to be in the Word more and have our kids devoted to it . . . since it truly can save our souls and provide hope and assurance even in the darkest of times. The hours and hours that David spent digging into the Bible over the years bore fruit—despite unfavorable circumstances.

Scripture Memory and Meditation

We believe that it is our job as parents to start training our children in the Word at a young age. My parents made Scripture study and memorization a staple in our household while we were growing up. At the time, I hated getting up early to have family "Wisdom Search." Now, looking back, I see that activity as one of the most meaningful times of my childhood—reading and discussing the Scriptures together, then kneeling as a family at the couch. I remember in first grade, my mom got me a Bible study workbook. We worked on it together each morning before the bus came to pick me up for school. Once we started homeschooling several years later, Scripture memory became a routine part of our day, and we memorized chapters and even entire books of the Bible. (Thank you, Mom. Sorry if I ever resisted this training.) This is the most priceless education that we could have ever received. Why? Because I now know that this is the only thing that remains—the Scriptures lodge deep within us and transform our soul.

When our kids were little, we played Scripture songs throughout the day and in their room at night while they were drifting to sleep. We now work to memorize key verses and entire chapters with our sons. It's amazing to witness them start to apply these verses to real-life scenarios and recall the verses at appropriate times. Children's minds are like sponges—they are capable of memorizing quickly and easily.

For us as adults, we might not have as sharp of a memory now as we used to, but that's not an excuse to not study and meditate on God's Word daily. Here are some ideas of how you can incorporate the Word of God into a daily practice:

- First, pray. Getting into God's Word is not easy because our enemy, the devil, does everything that he can to distract us and keep us away from it. You can expect a battle if you commit to making the study of the Bible a priority in your life. It can also be overwhelming to think about understanding what you are reading. Start by praying that God will give you an insatiable hunger for more of Him and more of His truth. Pray that the Holy Spirit will illuminate your thoughts and help you grasp and apply what it is that you are reading. Pray through every single step along the process of falling in love with the Word of God.

- Get a translation of the Bible that is accurate and easy to understand. We like the English Standard Version.

- If you read five Psalms a day or one Proverb a day, you'll finish each respective book within a month.

- You can pick any book to start with! You don't have to have a companion workbook to be a student of the Word—the Holy Spirit is our Teacher and will reveal truths to you as you commit yourself to seeking Him. Pray about where you're to start—maybe it's a New Testament book like John or Ephesians. Maybe it's the very beginning of the Bible, in Genesis. I also like to spend time each week studying the sermon notes and passages that were preached in church the Sunday before. This practice helps the message to lodge deeper into my heart and soul.

- Journal your thoughts, insights and questions as you read.

- Get involved in a Bible study or Bible-believing church to help you understand what you read and to have a safe space to ask questions. Learning together with other believers is incredibly powerful and effective.

- If you are a visual learner, draw pictures of what you are reading.

- If you are an auditory learner, read the Bible out loud or get an app that will read it out loud for you.

- Find a special place in your home or a safe place where you can consistently have your quiet time.

- Find the best time of day for you to study and learn. For me, it's early morning before anyone else wakes up.
- Believe in your heart of hearts that this sacred time is essential for your life! Distractions will come—expect them. Then hit them head-on with your reasons "why" spiritual investment in the Word is important enough to make happen.
- Grab an app, such as Tecarta Bible, or the *Strong's Concordance*, to quickly and easily look up the original meanings of the words.

A Personal Challenge

If you're not in God's Word daily, you are opening the door for sin to come into your home. I don't think any of us would say we want that. You've heard it said before, "Sin will keep you from the Word, or the Word will keep you from sin." I'm not asking you to be a biblical scholar that memorizes the whole Bible. If you can, that's awesome; I know of some who have done that! But just be in the Word, take time daily to study, and make it a priority. We make time for a lot of things such as going to the coffee shop or scrolling social media. We make time for whatever we want to do. Get in the Word of God as though your life depends on it, because it does.

Psalm 119:105 (ESV) says:

> *Your Word is a lamp to my feet and a light to my path.*

It's the light that guides us. Have you ever been out at night or the power goes out in your house and you don't have any light? You bump into stuff and stub your toe, and it hurts! We need light, and it's the light of Christ that guides and leads and directs and saves. The Word of God is truth. Proverbs 30:5a (ESV) says:

> *Every word of God proves true.*

> "Sin will keep you from the Word, or the Word will keep you from sin."

How much of it? Every word proves true, so get into the Word every day. I challenge you to examine your life. Put aside those things that don't matter and won't matter. Put Jesus Christ first, and seek Him for every decision, every dream, every desire, and every want.

Every day we are bombarded with messages from social media, television, radio, friends, etc. The majority of those messages contain relative truth, which means it changes frequently and doesn't last. Allowing these kinds of messages to consistently occupy our thoughts is, in fact, planting seeds which lead to stress and confusion. There is only one absolute truth that never changes—and that truth is the Word of God. It alone has the power to keep us grounded and give us hope, even in the now of a crazy, messed-up, and ever-changing world. You have the power to turn off the negative information from the world and turn to the life-giving, life-changing Word of God.

This wonderful Bible, with all its sixty-six books written over 2,000 years ago by various authors from various continents, points to one Savior, Jesus Christ. When life happens, where do we turn? When trials come, do we say, "Why me? Why is this happening to me? Why not somebody else?" If so, we need to instead say, "Lord, Your will and Your way, even though it's scary, and even though we don't know what the next days are going to bring. When we don't know why things are playing out the way they are (knowing why is often above our pay grade), we don't have to know; we just have to be obedient.

As you continue on your journey to see God's Word come alive in your life, we'd love to stay in touch and hear from you. Please snap a picture of your Bible, post it on social media and tag us with the #OneThingRemainsForMe hashtag.

This experience shook us and broke us. Every single aspect of life was affected and altered. Walking through those long twenty-six days, there were moments that we didn't know when—or if—the miraculous end would ever come. We hoped and prayed for a miracle, but also knew that we had been promised suffering in life as well. This was uncharted territory, and we were scared.

Thankfully, by the grace of God, we didn't become bitter in the journey.

Broken and crushed, yes.

Exposed, yes.

Vulnerable and unsure, yes.

But we had an anchor that carried us.

Often we remarked, "How do people walk through suffering without knowing the strength and peace of God?" We still don't have an answer for that. All we know is that He never left us. Even in the midst of a million unknowns, we knew that He was still God. We had a spark of hope—not just wishful thinking, but a true assurance that, no matter what, we were going to be OK. And not just OK—God would use this experience for a remarkable life-shift in our family.

> *He used all of it to wake us up, to get our attention . . . and to embrace what really matters.*

It's strange to say—but we thanked Him during and we thanked Him after the trial for the privilege of encountering amnesia. Without it, we shudder to think about how we'd still be stuck on the hamster wheel of chaos and stress. He used all of it to wake us up, to get our attention . . . and to embrace what really matters.

The last sermon David preached prior to his memory loss was on 1 Corinthians 2. We'd encourage you to go read the entire chapter in light of all that you've learned through this book. Truly, God used the "foolish" (bizarre and weak) things of the world to confound the wise. He stripped and humbled us of all that we thought that mattered in order to show us that He alone is enough. For many of us, it takes times of suffering to get to the point of declaring with Paul (1 Cor. 2:2 ESV):

> For I decided to know nothing among you except Jesus Christ and him crucified.

And we love how 1 Corinthians 2 (ESV) ends:

But we have the mind of Christ!

We can tell you from personal experience, you don't have to have all your memories to still have access through the Spirit to the mind of Christ.

We asked the boys what they learned from all that we walked through with their dad's amnesia. Reid said, "He remembered everything from the Bible, which was pretty wild." Caleb remarked, "I learned that, even though my dad was scared, he kept pushing through. It taught me that fear is pointless sometimes." And Evan interjected this profound summary, "He made some pretty good food during that time . . . his cheeseburgers were excellent."

REFLECTION PRAYER

Heavenly Father, thank You for Your Word, which I'm learning has incredible power to reach the depths of my being. I praise You for the eternal, living, active nature of Your Word. Thank You for this gift that leads and guides me through this life. Forgive me for making other things that won't last more of a priority. Help me to develop a passion for Your Word and make it my first go-to for every situation in life. Give me a hunger to go deeper in Your Word every day, knowing that this action alone has the life-changing power to transform my entire life and mind.

Epilogue

Over a year has come and gone since our lives were turned upside down by this story. We are still gripped by how it broke and changed us in countless ways. Even though we sometimes still cry as we relive and continue to heal from heart-wrenching, painful moments from that season, we also look back with a heart of gratitude for *all* of it.

One of the things that we often share with the church is that we are to give God credit and praise for every situation in life. It should always be on our lips, "Look what the Lord has done." If your heart is surrendered to Him, you can be assured that He is working overtime on your behalf. He is continually transforming and shaping you to look more like Himself. Maybe this story has helped you see that even the bizarre and painful circumstances you are in could actually be tools God will use for your good. We might not always understand it all; we just need to be faithful. This reality is the heart of **Life-Changing Lesson 1: Suffering is normal.**

We did put our homestead on the market and, after it sold, moved into a much-smaller home in a cute neighborhood. We downsized over 1,700 square feet and many acres—yet we are at peace and extremely happy in our new home. Everyone in the family comments almost daily about how much we love this home and our more relaxed pace. David often says that sometimes we don't realize the bondage we are in until afterwards, when we are removed from the situation. The homestead was a beautiful part of our story, but the season for that lifestyle passed—

and our spirits recognized that it was time for something else. We truly internalized the **Life-Changing Lesson 2: God doesn't want us to live a stress-filled life.**

We miss our chickens, but we know they are in good hands. We have taken some time off from gardening, but plan to build and plant raised beds next season. We are excited to support local farmers' markets this year for our fresh produce.

It's amazing to see how the long-term commitment to **Life-Changing Lesson 3** has remained in our family: **It is possible to have a reset in your relationships and live with a clean slate.** We are eternally grateful to God for the reset that He gave us and the renewed joy and unity we have in our marriage!

David returned to pastoring full time a couple of months after his miraculous healing. Thank you to our church for recognizing that he needed a little extra time to heal and figure out what life and ministry would look like going forward. Relationships with those in our church are even stronger after walking through this experience together. No church is perfect and ours has had its share of bumps and bruises. But we press on and are excited about the ministry opportunities that await this dedicated and godly group of believers! **Life-Changing Lesson 4 is true: Community is a gift from God.**

As we wrote this book, we were forced to revisit these five life-changing lessons we learned from amnesia. Many of the changes that we have written about have been deeply implanted in us and remained—praise God! But we also had to take a dose of our own medicine as we poured over these chapters. We realized that, in some areas, we had quietly slipped back into some forms of unnecessary busyness and not managing stress well. The words in this book preached to us, and we—like you might have—had to stop and do some evaluating.

This life is a journey for all of us. Thankfully, we aren't the family we used to be, but we aren't yet the family that we want to be either. If you're like us and you at least want to grow and be transformed, and you desire simplicity and embracing what really matters, then you're exactly where you need to be.

> Remember not the former things,
> nor consider the things of old.
> Behold, I am doing a new thing;
> NOW it springs forth, do you not perceive it?
> — Isaiah 43:18–19a (ESV, emphasis added)

Ultimately, our lives continue to be gripped by the power of God's Word and we are propelled forward with the **Life-Changing Lesson 5: God's Word prevails and remains**. It is our family's urgent mission to help equip Christians to be students of the Word, especially in these uncertain and troubling times.

We hope that you'll continue to connect with us and share your stories of how this book led to your own life-changing lessons and journey. We'd love to hear your takeaways and how the message of this book has impacted your life. If you are on social media, we'd be honored for you to post your thoughts and takeaways and tag us using the #OneThingRemainsForMe hashtag. You can find us on Instagram @davidandshannoncarroll. We also have many more resources for you online at www.DavidAndShannonCarroll.com.

REVIEW REQUEST

Hey, it's David and Shannon here.

We hope that you've enjoyed our story, finding it both thought-provoking and life-changing. We have a favor to ask you.

Would you consider giving this book a rating wherever you bought it? Online bookstores are more likely to promote a book when they feel good about its content, and reader reviews are a great barometer for a book's quality.

So please go to the website of wherever you bought your copy, search for our names and the book title, and leave a review. If able, perhaps consider adding a picture of you holding the book. That increases the likelihood that your review will be accepted!

Many thanks in advance,

David and Shannon Carroll
#OneThingRemainsForMe

WILL YOU SHARE THE LOVE?

Get this book for a friend, associate, or family member!

If you have found this book valuable and know others who would find it useful, consider buying them a copy as a gift. Special bulk discounts are available if you would like your whole team, organization, or church to benefit from reading this true story.
Just contact us through our website at
www.DavidAndShannonCarroll.com.

WOULD YOU LIKE DAVID AND SHANNON CARROLL TO SPEAK TO YOUR ORGANIZATION, GROUP OR CHURCH?

Book David and Shannon now!

David and Shannon accept a limited number of speaking and training engagements each year. To learn how you can bring their message to your organization, group or church, email them at **David@DavidAndShannonCarroll.com** or **Shannon@DavidAndShannonCarroll.com.**

About the Authors

David and Shannon Carroll live in Southern Indiana with their three boys and a dog. David is the pastor of a growing, thriving church and Shannon runs a home-based wellness business while homeschooling their two younger boys. They love to minister together through their dynamic gifts of preaching, teaching, and music, telling their stories and all the ways that God has been faithful to them, in spite of them. People are drawn to their real and raw messages of trials and triumph, where they direct others back to the truths of God's Word and how it applies practically in all areas of life today. In their free time, they love to travel, take walks, and try new recipes with their family.

David and Shannon can be reached at:
www.DavidAndShannonCarroll.com.

Made in the USA
Monee, IL
22 October 2020